THE PRINCIPLES OF
BEAUTIFUL
WEB DESIGN

BY JASON BEAIRD

Copyright © 2007 SitePoint Pty. Ltd.

Expert Reviewer: Andy Rutledge   **Managing Editor:** Simon Mackie
Technical Editor: Craig Anderson   **Technical Director:** Kevin Yank
Editor: Georgina Laidlaw   **Index Editor:** Nigel d'Auvergne
Cover Design: Jess Mason   **Cover Layout:** Alex Walker
Production: *Book*NZ (www.booknz.co.nz)

Printing History
First Edition: January 2007   **Reprinted:** March 2008

Published by SitePoint Pty. Ltd.
48 Cambridge Street Collingwood
VIC Australia 3066.
Web: www.sitepoint.com
Email: business@sitepoint.com

ISBN 978-0-9802858-9-5
Printed and bound in Canada

*To my wife Amy, who inspires me every day to reach for my goals
no matter how unprepared I am for them when I get there.
You truly are my better half.*

*To my mom and dad.
You have no idea how much the craft shows, cereal box animals,
and driftwood paintings have contributed to my creativity.*

*To Nathan, Ryan, and Russ, "The Programmers" at Acceleration.
Your random color choices and offbeat design decisions
are the inspiration for this book.*

About the Author

"Jason the Designer Man," as one of his coworkers once called him, dual-majored in graphic design and digital media at the University of Central Florida.

When he's not working on web sites, he enjoys disassembling electronics and using them in his artwork. Jason writes about his adventures in design and technology on his personal site.[1]

About the Expert Reviewer

Andy Rutledge is a designer and composer from Texas. His design passions include web design, information architecture, web standards, usability, and professionalism-related issues in the design community, and he writes about these topics on his personal site.[2] Andy is creative director for NetSuccess in Dallas, Texas.[3]

About the Technical Editor

Craig plays bass guitar in Melbourne rock band *Look Who's Toxic*,[4] and indulges in all the extracurricular activities you'd expect of a computer nerd/musician approaching 30 (other than role playing—somehow he never got into that).

About the Technical Director

As Technical Director for SitePoint, Kevin Yank oversees all of its technical publications— books, articles, newsletters, and blogs. He has written over 50 articles for SitePoint, but is best known for his book, *Build Your Own Database Driven Website Using PHP & MySQL*. Kevin lives in Melbourne, Australia, and enjoys performing improvised comedy theatre and flying light aircraft.

About SitePoint

SitePoint specializes in publishing fun, practical, and easy-to-understand content for web professionals. Visit http://www.sitepoint.com to access our books, newsletters, articles, and community forums.

---

1   http://www.jasongraphix.com/
2   http://www.andyrutledge.com/
3   http://www.netsuccess.com/
4   http://www.lookwhostoxic.com/

Acknowledgements

Thanks to Simon Mackie for asking me to write this book, and for all the encouragement he offered along the way. Thanks to Andy Rutledge for keeping the content realistic with constructive criticism and professional insight. Thanks to Craig Anderson for his technical feedback and grammatical wizardry. Thanks to Georgina Laidlaw who made sure I crossed my ts and dotted my is. Thanks to Malcolm Whild for arranging my bits and bytes onto these beautiful pages. Thanks to my family and friends, who pushed me forward by constantly asking, "How's it coming along?" Finally, respect and highest regards to all the talented designers whose work is featured in this book. Your passion and ingenuity are what make this a topic worth writing about.

Table of Contents

Preface

When my wife and I moved into our house, one of our first major projects was to update the bathroom. The horribly gaudy floral wallpaper pattern, in combination with the gold sink fixtures, obnoxious mirrors, and tacky lighting, made us feel like we'd stepped into a previous decade every time we entered the master bathroom. Removing wallpaper is a tough job, but it's even more difficult when there are multiple layers of the stuff. This was the case with our bathroom. Apparently the previous homeowners' taste in wallpaper changed every few years, and rather than stripping off the wallpaper and starting over, they just covered ugly with more ugly. Ah, the joys of home ownership!

If there's one thing our renovation adventures have taught me, it's that there are strong parallels between designing a room's decor and designing a good web site.

■ **Good design is about the relationships between the elements involved, and creating a balance between them.**

Whether we're talking about a web site or bathroom makeover, throwing up a new layer of wallpaper or changing the background color isn't a design solution in itself—it's just part of a solution. While we removed the wallpaper and rollered some paint onto our bathroom, we also had to change the light fixtures, remove the gold shower doors, replace the mirrors, upgrade the lighting, paint the cabinets, change the switches and plugs, and scrape off the popcorn ceilings. If we'd just removed the tacky wallpaper and left all the other stuff, we'd still have an outdated bathroom. Web site design is similar: you can only do so many minor updates before the time comes to scrap what you have and start over.

■ **Fads come and go, but good design is timeless.**

Conforming to the latest design trends is a good way to ensure temporary public appeal, but how long will those trends last? As far as I know, there was hardly ever a time when **marquee** and **blink** tags were accepted as professional web design markup ... but scrolling JavaScript news tickers, "high readability" hit-counters, and chunky table borders have graced the homepages of many high-profile sites in the past. These are the shag carpets, sparkly popcorn ceilings, and faux wood paneling of the web design world. Take a trip in the Internet Wayback Machine, and look for mid-'90s versions of some of the top Fortune 500 and pre-dot-com-boom-era web sites.[5] Try to find examples of good and bad design. In the midst of some of the most outdated web sites, you're likely to find some designs that still look good. Most likely, those graphical elements weren't dependent on the "cutting edge" filters in what, at the time, was the recently released Photoshop 4.0. Good design transcends technology.

---

5   http://www.archive.org

■ The finishing touches make a big impression.

I've heard it argued recently that deep down, people really love "anti-marketing design." The idea is that we trust sites that have an unpolished appearance and don't feel professional. I think this argument misses the point. No matter what type of web site you're developing, the design should be as intentional as the functionality. My wife and I didn't change the functionality of our bathroom with the work that we did. We just fine-tuned the details, but they made a world of difference. Some people might have been able to live with the bathroom the way it was, but I doubt you'd find anyone who would say it was exactly what they wanted. Similarly, if you're spending time developing a web site, you should take time to design it. Under no circumstances should the design feel unpolished or haphazard. If you want to come off as anti-marketing and non-corporate, then do that, and do it well—but there's no reason to be ignorant about, or feel intimidated by, design.

My goal with this book is simple: To present what I know about design in a way that anyone can understand and apply. Why? Because the basics of web site design should be common knowledge. We all live in and work on an Internet that has been blindly covering up ugly with more ugly since its inception. It's time to break that chain and make bold moves toward better design.

Who Should Read this Book?

If you are squeamish about choosing colors, feel uninspired by a blank browser window, or get lost trying to choose the right font, this book is for you. In it, I take a methodical approach to presenting traditional graphic design theory as it applies to today's web site development industry. While the content is directed toward programmers and developers, it provides a design primer that will benefit readers at any level.

What's in this Book?

■ Chapter 1: Layout and Composition

An awareness of design relies heavily on understanding the spatial relationships that exist between the individual components of a design. The layout chapter kicks off the design process by investigating possible page components. With these blocks defined, we discuss some tools and examples that will help you start your own designs on a solid foundation. Finally, we commence the development of a layout for our sample web site design, which we'll build on throughout the book.

■ Chapter 2: Color

Perhaps the most mysterious aspect of design is the topic of color selection. Chapter 2 sheds some light on this topic as we delve into both the aesthetic and scientific aspects of color theory. Armed with these simple guidelines, and some tips for creating harmonious color combinations, anybody can choose a set of colors that work well together to complement the overall message of a web site. We'll do just that toward the end of the chapter, when we select a relevant and attractive palette for our sample web site design.

■ Chapter 3: Texture

An aspect of web design that's often overlooked, texture is the key to creating designs that stand out. By understanding how the individual elements of texture function, you'll learn how to use points, lines, and shapes to communicate and support your site's message on a number of levels. We'll then apply what we've learned to the sample site layout, which will give us a chance to see firsthand just how much value texture can add to the overall impact of a web site design.

■ Chapter 4: Typography

The importance of typography is self-evident. Type is everywhere, and understanding the mechanics of written language is essential for any visual designer. In this chapter, we'll dive beneath the surface of this rich topic, exploring the basics of the letterform, and investigating various typeface distinctions. When the time comes, you'll have the opportunity to get your hands dirty as we apply carefully selected typefaces to our sample site design.

 Chapter 5: Imagery

The necessary companions to any well-designed site are the images and illustrations that grace its pages. In the final chapter, we'll discuss what we should look for in the visual elements that we use on our pages, and locate sources of legitimate supporting imagery. Of course, finding the right image is often just the beginning. We'll also learn the basics of cropping, masking, borders, and file formats, before we take the final step in our sample site design: incorporating imagery that supports our clients' branding, and helps communicate the message they're trying to convey.

This Book's Web Site

Located at http://www.sitepoint.com/books/design1/, the web site that supports this book will give you access to the following facilities.

Updates and Errata

The Corrections and Typos page on the book's web site, at http://www.sitepoint.com/books/design1/errata.php, will always have the latest information about known typographical and code errors, and necessary updates that reflect changes to technologies.

The SitePoint Forums

While I've made every attempt to anticipate the questions you may have, and answer them in this book, there is no way that any publication could cover everything there is to know about web design. If you have a question about anything in this book, the best place to go for a quick answer is the SitePoint Forums—SitePoint's vibrant and knowledgeable community.[6]

The SitePoint Newsletters

In addition to books like this one, SitePoint offers free email newsletters. The *SitePoint Tech Times* covers the latest news, product releases, trends, tips, and techniques for all technical aspects of web development. The long-running *SitePoint Tribune* is a biweekly digest of the business and moneymaking aspects of the Web. Whether you're a freelance developer looking for tips to score that dream contract, or a marketing major striving to

---

6   http://www.sitepoint.com/forums/

keep abreast of changes to the major search engines, this is the newsletter for you. The *SitePoint Design View* is a monthly compilation of the best in web design. From new CSS layout methods to subtle Photoshop techniques, SitePoint's chief designer shares his years of experience in its pages. Browse the archives or sign up to any of SitePoint's free newsletters at http://www.sitepoint.com/newsletter/.

Your Feedback

If you can't find your answer through the forums, or you wish to contact me for any other reason, the best place to write is books@sitepoint.com. SitePoint has a well-manned email support system set up to track your inquiries, and if the support staff are unable to answer your question, they send it straight to me. Suggestions for improvement as well as notices of any mistakes you may find are especially welcome.

CHAPTER 1

Layout and Composition

For many web developers, myself included, the most intimidating part of the design process is getting started. Imagine for a moment that you're sitting at your desk with nothing other than a cup of coffee and the business card of a potential client who needs a basic corporate web site. Usually, a business card speaks volumes about a company's identity, and could be used as design inspiration.

Unfortunately, that's not the case with the card for Smith Services in Figure 1.1. It's black and white, all text, no character, blah. Talk about a blank canvas! So, where do you go from here? You need a plan … and you need to contact Mr. Smith. With some critical input from the client about what his company actually *does*, and by gathering information about the content you have to work with, you'll be able to come up with a successful layout and design.

**SMITH'S
SERVICES**

Jim Smith
Professional Service Associate

100 Random Street
Suite 16
Somewhere, VA 54321

Tel. 867-5309
Fax. 555-2368

Figure 1.1: A bland client business card

Anyone, no matter what level of artistic talent he or she has, can come up with a design that works well and looks good—all it takes is a little experience and a working knowledge of some basic layout principles. So let's get started with the basics and before long you'll have the foundation necessary to design gallery-quality web sites.

The Design Process

In a web-programming book I read recently, the author introduced a fictional scenario to explain why readers needed to design a page layout and create a style sheet for the example application. He basically said that the company web designer was off getting inspiration from somewhere and wouldn't be back until later in the year. It sounded as if he was implying that designers are prone to flake out and go on vision quests for months at a time, but I'm going to assume the author made that comment in an endearing way, and introduce the same scenario.

Here are the hypothetical details of this scenario: Jim Smith of Smith Services needs a web site. We have his business card and he's eager to get started. Unfortunately, the designer is out of town … wait, that's not a good excuse. Let's say he was injured during a freak dairy cow stampede while attending the South by South West Interactive (SXSWi) festival in Austin, Texas. Yeah, that's believable. Anyway, he's out for a few months, and you're on your own. So where do you start? The actual process of developing an entire site or web application includes a lot of steps, but the process of creating a design comp boils down to only two tasks: discovery and implementation.

Discovery

The discovery component of the design process is about meeting the clients and discovering what they do. This may not feel like a "designy" task, but gathering information about who your clients are and how they run their business is the only way you'll be able to come up with an appropriate and effective design.

Before you schedule your first meeting with your clients, take a few minutes to figure out what they do and how they do it. If they've asked you to design a web site for them, they may not currently have one, but Google them anyway. If you can't find any information about their business specifically, try to learn a little more about their industry before the first meeting. Whenever possible, the first meeting with a client should be an actual person-to-person meeting. Sometimes, distance will dictate that the initial meeting will occur over the phone, but if the client is in town, schedule a time to meet.

Keep in mind that this meeting isn't about impressing the client, selling yourself, or

> **NOTE   What's a Comp?**
>
> The word **comp** is an abbreviation of the phrase comprehensive dummy, and is a term that comes from the print design world. It's a complete simulation of a printed layout that's created before the layout goes to press. In translating this term to web design, a comp is an image of a layout that's created before we begin to prototype the design in HTML.

selling a web site. The initial client meeting is about communication. Try to listen more than you speak, and bring a pad of paper on which you can make notes. *Do not* bring a laptop. Computers have screens, and people tend to stare at them. If the client isn't staring at the screen the whole time, you will be as you write your notes. If you must drag some technology into the meeting, bring a voice recorder. In my experience, though, a pad of paper is less threatening to the often not-so-tech-savvy client.

> **TIP** *Client Meetings don't have to Take Place in an Office*
>
> Even when I worked for a company with a big office, I had some of my most productive client meetings at a coffeehouse or over lunch. The feasibility of this approach depends on the client. If your contact doesn't seem like the informal meeting type, don't suggest it; in many cases, though, it's a good way to make a business meeting more personal.

Here are a few of the questions I like to ask in initial client meetings even if I've already answered them myself via a search engine:

- What does the company do?
- What is your role in the company?[1]
- Does the company have an existing logo or brand?
- What is your goal in developing a web site?
- What information do you wish to provide online?
- Who comprises your target audience? Do its members share any common demographics, like age, sex, or a physical location?
- Who are your competitors and do they have web sites?

Sometimes I start off with more questions than those listed here—use your imagination and try to come up with some creative queries that will really give you more insight into the client organization. If you're a programmer, avoid the tech jargon. If you're a designer, avoid talking specifically about design. Sure, that may be all you're thinking about, but semantic markup, fluid and fixed layouts, and color schemes will likely mean very little to the client. Worse still, these types of conversations can bring misguided design opinions your way even before you get a chance to start thinking about the design yourself.

Implementation

The next step in the design process is to take what you've learned from the client and use it to create a design. Regardless of the project, try not to get caught up in the technology associated with building web sites—at least not at first. At this point, it shouldn't matter whether the site is going to comprise straight HTML, a template for a content management system, or a Ruby on Rails application; the bottom line is that we have an interface to

---

1   This question is especially important if this person is going to be your main point of contact.

design and a blank sheet of paper. "Paper?" That's right, paper. Did you really think I was going to let you get back to your precious computer right after the client meeting was over? No way. Here's why: it's easy to lose focus on the design if you start thinking about the layout in front of a computer. If you start out on paper, you can ignore the technical limitations of browsers and CSS, and focus on how you want the final product to look. Now you might think that all good designers carry around fancy hardbound sketch books in which they use expensive markers and paint to design masterpiece renderings of web page layouts. For me, the equivalent is a 79¢ spiral-bound notebook and any writing instrument I can find on my desk that still works.

I start out by sketching a few possible layouts. After a few of these sketches, I decide on one I like, jump into Photoshop, and use the rectangle tool to block out the areas I've marked down on my paper. Once I've defined my layout, I experiment with foreground and background colors until I have a solid color scheme. I continue twiddling the Photoshop knobs and pushing around pixels until, finally, I have a comp to show the client.

Simple, right? Okay, perhaps I skipped a few steps in that brief description. Honestly, though, when people ask me how I do what I do, they usually get a similar explanation. The truth is that there are bundles of now-subconscious information from my past experience and those old college design and art classes that have helped me to define my own design process.

Learning how to design is like learning how to program. Some people have a bit of a knack for it, but anyone can learn. Just as there is good code and ugly code, there is good design and ugly design. Learning some of the principles and conventions that are associated with design will help you to understand the difference between the good and the ugly, and help you toward establishing your own design process.

Defining Good Design

There are two main standpoints from which most people determine whether a web site design is "good" or "bad." There's a strict usability standpoint, which focuses on functionality, the effective presentation of information, and efficiency. Then there's the purely aesthetic perspective, which is all about presentation, hot animations, and sexy graphics. Some designers get caught up in the aesthetics and graphics and forget about the user, and some usability gurus get lost in their user testing and forget about visual appeal. In order to reach people *and* retain their interest, it's essential to maximize both.

The most important thing to keep in mind is that design is about communication. If you create a web site that works and presents information well, but looks ugly or doesn't fit with the client's brand, no one will want to use it. Similarly, if you make a beautiful web site that isn't usable and accessible, people may not be able to use it. Indeed, the elements and functionality of a finished web site design should work as a single cohesive unit, so that:

■ **Users are pleased by the design but drawn to the content**

One of the biggest concerns among usability professionals is the time it takes users to scan the page for the information they want, be it a piece of content, a link to another page, or a form field. The design should not be a hindrance; it should act as a conduit between the user and the information.

John Oxton's Bus Full of Hippies template[2] (pictured in Figure 1.2) is a great example of a design that's both beautiful and usable. The colorful graphics grow around the blocks of content, leading the eye back to the information without interfering with the pages' readability or organization.

Figure 1.2: The Bus Full of Hippies template

■ **Users can move about easily via intuitive navigation**

We'll talk more about the placement of navigation later, but the main navigation block itself should be clearly visible on the page, and each link should have a descriptive title. A navigation structure that not only changes appearance on mouse hover, but also indicates the active page or section, as does the menu shown in Figure 1.3, helps users recognize where they are, and how to get where they want to go.

Figure 1.3: A navigation menu from Iconfactory's Halloween 2006 theme[3]

Secondary navigation, search fields, and outgoing links should not be dominant features of the page. If we make these items easy to find, and separate them visually from the content, we allow users to focus on the information, though they'll know where to look when they're ready to move on to other content.

Users recognize each page as belonging to the site

Even if there's a dramatic difference between the layout of the homepage and the rest of the site, a cohesive theme or style should exist across all the pages of a site to help hold the design together.

Take a look at the screenshots of Steve Smith's Ordered List in Figure 1.4.[4] Although the content blocks on these pages are divided differently, there are several visual indicators that let users know that these are pages from the same site. Much of this unity is due to the repetition of the identity and navigation blocks. The consistent use of a very limited color palette (black, white, green, and cyan) also helps to unify the pages.

Figure 1.4: Pages from Ordered List

---

3   http://iconfactory.com/
4   http://orderedlist.com/

Web Page Anatomy

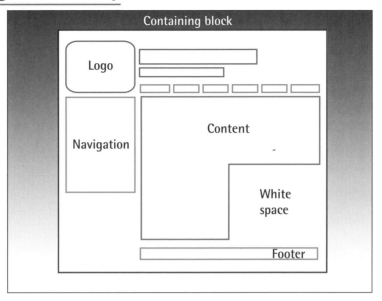

Figure 1.5: The anatomy of a web page

Even from a non-designer's standpoint, defining a design that satisfies all of the requirements I outlined above is a simple task. It's similar to making a phrase on your refrigerator with magnetic poetry words. Although there are millions of ways to arrange the words, only a few arrangements make any sense. The magnetic poetry words are like the components, or blocks, of the web page. Although the number of these necessary blocks depends on the size and subject of the site, most web sites have the following components, as shown in Figure 1.5.

■ **Containing Block**

Every web page has a container. This could be in the form of the page's **body** tag, an all-containing **div** tag, or (and I really don't want to say this, but) a **table**. Without some sort of container, we would have no place to put the contents of our page. The elements would drift beyond the bounds of our browser window and off into empty space. The width of the container can be **liquid**, meaning it expands to fill the width of the browser window; or **fixed**, so that the content is the same width no matter what size the window is.

■ **Logo**

When designers refer to an identity, they're referring to the logo and colors that exist across a company's various forms of marketing, such as business cards, letterhead, brochures, and so on.[5]

The identity block that appears on the web site should contain the company's logo or name, and sit at the top of each page of the web site. The identity block increases brand recognition and lets users know that the pages they're viewing are part of a single site.

■ Navigation

It's essential that the site's navigation system is easy to find and use. Users expect to see navigation right at the top of the page. Whether you plan to use vertical menus down the side of the page, or a horizontal menu along the page's top, the navigation should be as close to the top of the layout as possible. At the very least, all main navigation items should appear "above the fold."

> **NOTE   Above the Fold**
>
> The **fold**, as some usability experts call it, is the end of the content users can see on a page before they scroll down. This metaphor is derived from the concept of a fold in a newspaper. If you look at the cover of a folded newspaper, most of the headlines and important news will appear on the top half, so that you can see the most important news items at a glance when the newspaper is folded. The location of the fold on a web page depends on the browser dimensions and the user's screen resolution. At a resolution of 800 × 600 pixels, accounting for browser chrome, the address bar, and a bottom status bar, the fold is usually just over 400 pixels from the top.

■ Content

Content is king. A typical web site visitor will enter and leave a web site in a matter of seconds. If visitors can't find what they're looking for, they will undoubtedly close the browser or move on to another site. It's important to keep the main content block as the focal point of a design so that precious seconds aren't wasted as visitors scan the page for the information they need.

■ Footer

Located at the bottom of the page, the footer usually contains copyright, contact, and legal information, as well as a few links to the main sections of the site.

By separating the end content from the bottom of the browser window, the footer should indicate to users that they're at the bottom of the page.

■ Whitespace

The graphic design term **whitespace** (or **negative space**) literally refers to any area of a page that's not covered by type or illustrations. While many novice web designers (and most clients) feel a need to fill every inch of a web page with photos, text, tables, and data, having empty space on a page is every bit as important as having content. Without carefully planned whitespace, a design will feel closed in, like a crowded room. Whitespace helps a design to "breathe" by guiding the user's eye around a page, but also helps to create balance and unity—two important concepts that we'll discuss in more detail later in this chapter.

---

5   Many people use the words identity and branding interchangeably. Branding is a broad term that describes the process of developing an awareness of a company, product, or service. The branding process involves advertising, market research, customer feedback, and much more. Identity is actually a subset of branding in that it deals only with the visual aspects of branding.

At this point, we've had our initial meeting with Mr. Smith, our theoretical client, and it was very helpful. He explained very thoroughly what he does and what he wants the site to achieve. Even though we don't have actual content yet, we can use the standard blocks of web page anatomy to start developing a layout. Although other site-specific blocks are worked into the designs of many web site layouts, the web page anatomy works to summarize the most common blocks.

Now that we have this information, how can we use it to create a foundational layout for Smith's Services? It's time for some grid theory.

Grid Theory

When most people think about grids, they think about engineering and architecture. However, the grid is an essential tool for graphic design as well.

Using a grid is not just about making things be square and line up: it's about proportion as well. That's where the "theory" comes into grid theory. Many art historians credit Dutch painter Piet Mondrian as the father of graphic design for his sophisticated use of grids. Yet classical grid theory has influenced successful artistic efforts for thousands of years. The concept of dividing the elements of a composition extends back to the mathematical ideas established by Pythagoras and his followers, who defined numbers as ratios rather than single units.

The Pythagoreans observed a mathematical pattern that occurred so often in nature that they believed it to be divinely inspired. They referred to this pattern as the **golden ratio** or **divine proportion**. The basic idea is illustrated in Figure 1.6. A line can be bisected using the golden ratio by dividing its length by 1.62. This magical 1.62 number is really 1.6180339 … It's an irrational number that's usually represented as Φ (pronounced phi). Explaining the math used to come up with this number is a bit too involved for this discussion, and isn't really going to help you become a better designer, so I'll spare you the details. Besides, my math is a little rusty.

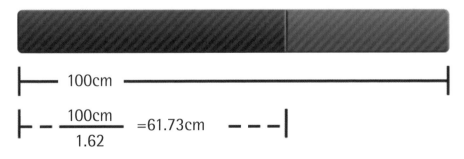

Figure 1.6: The golden ratio

This sunflower is an example of golden ratio in nature. The diameter of the center of the sunflower is the total diameter of the sunflower, including the petals, divided by Φ.

So just what does this ratio have to do with graphic design? In general, compositions divided by lines that are proportionate to the golden ratio are considered to be aesthetically pleasing. The artists of the Renaissance used divine proportion to design their paintings, sculpture, and architecture, just as designers today often employ this ratio when creating page layouts, posters, and brochures. Rather than relying on artistic notion, divine proportion gives us logical guidelines for producing appealing layouts.

The Rule of Thirds

A simplified version of the golden ratio is the **rule of thirds**, or in the native accent of one of my graphic design professors, "rule of turds." A line bisected by the golden ratio is divided into two sections, one of which is approximately twice the size of the other. Dividing a composition into thirds is an easy way to apply divine proportion without getting out your calculator.

To start the pencil-and-paper version of your layout, draw a rectangle. The vertical and horizontal dimensions don't really matter, but try to keep straight lines and 90-degree angles.

Now, divide your rectangle horizontally and vertically by thirds. As I said before, don't start thinking about technology yet.

Next, divide the top third of your layout into thirds again.

Finally, divide each of your columns in half to create a little more of a grid.

You should have a square on your paper that looks similar to the rule of thirds grid in the final diagram of Figure 1.7. Go ahead and repeat the above steps so that you have a few rule of thirds grids in which to try different layout options.

With this simple gridwork in place, we can begin to lay out our elements. The large, main rectangle represents the container that we talked about in the section called "Web Page Anatomy." When using this method of layout design, I like to place the biggest block first. Usually, that block represents the content. In my first rule-of-thirds

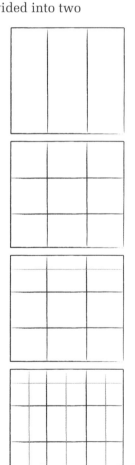

Figure 1.7: A grid created using the rule of thirds

grid, I place the content block within the two-thirds of the layout at the lower right. Next, I place my navigation block in the middle third of the left-hand column. I place the text part of the identity block over the left side of the content, and the image part of the identity over the menu. Finally, I squash the copyright block below the content, in the right-hand column of the grid. The result is the top-left of the four possible layout arrangements shown in Figure 1.8.

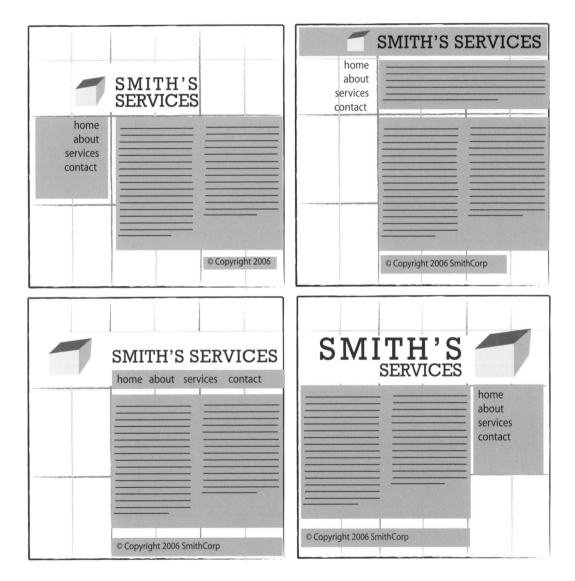

Figure 1.8: Four layouts in grids that follow the rule of thirds

As you experiment with different arrangements, use the lines that create the three main columns as alignment guides for the identity, navigation, content, and footer blocks. It's very tempting to arrange all your elements along one particular line, but try not to let this happen—it's not very interesting visually. Instead, consider pushing part of the block over that line, as I did with the identity block in the examples in Figure 1.8.

Another tendency for non-designers working on layouts is to center-align everything on a page. The grid system prevents us from doing that, but there is a reason why we tend to want to center everything. That reason is a desire for **balance**.

Balance

In a figurative sense, the concept of visual balance is similar to that of physical balance illustrated by a seesaw. Just as physical objects have weight, so do the elements of a layout. If the elements on either side of a layout are of equal weight, they balance one another. There are two main forms of visual balance: symmetrical and asymmetrical.

Symmetrical Balance

Symmetrical balance, or formal balance, occurs when the elements of a composition are the same on either side of an axis line. The digital painting *Contemplation* by David Lanham, shown in Figure 1.9, is a great example of this concept. Notice how the male and female figures in this painting are almost the same in position and proportion. Even the shaded background boxes are mirror images of one another.

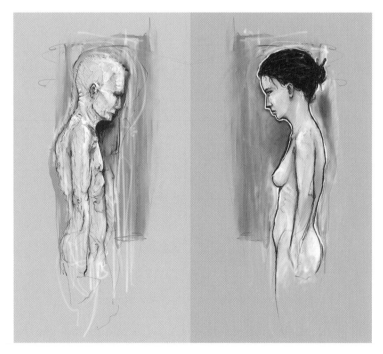

Figure 1.9: Symmetrical balance—*Contemplation* by David Lanham[6]

Although it may not be practical for all designs and clients, this type of symmetry—called **horizontal symmetry**—can be applied to web site layouts by centering content or balancing it between columns. The Grow Collective web site is an example of such symmetry.[7] Notice on the page shown in Figure 1.10 that the content areas graduate from a single column at the very top of the page, to two columns, to three columns at the bottom of the window; yet the layout still maintains its symmetrical balance. Most of the rest of the site's content is divided into symmetrical columns as well.

Figure 1.10: Grow Collective web page

The two other forms of symmetrical balance are less common in web site design, due to the nature of the medium. However, they're commonly exhibited in logo and print design. These are:

- **bilateral symmetry**, which exists when a composition is balanced on more than one axis
- **radial symmetry**, which occurs when elements are equally spaced around a central point

---

7   http://gr0w.com/

Asymmetrical Balance

Asymmetrical balance, or informal balance, is a little more abstract, and generally more visually interesting, than symmetrical balance. Rather than having mirror images on either side of the layout, asymmetrical balance involves objects of differing size, shape, tone, or placement. These objects are arranged so that, despite their differences, they equalize the weight of the page. If you have a large object on one side of a page, and you partner it with several smaller items on the other side, the composition can still feel balanced.

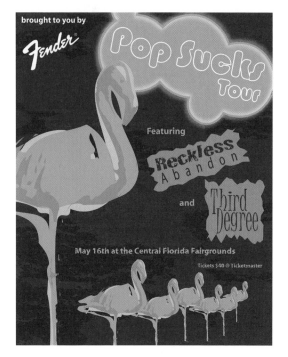

Figure 1.11: Asymmetrically balanced design by Jeremy Darty

Figure 1.12: Asymmetrical rocks that don't roll

The concert poster by my friend Jeremy Darty presented in Figure 1.11 is a fine example of asymmetrical balance. The visual weight of the large pink flamingo on the left is balanced by the combined weight of the smaller flamingos and small text blocks on the right-hand side of the layout. Notice also Jeremy's use of the rule of thirds. The blue cloud behind the Pop Sucks title takes up one-third of the vertical space and spans two-thirds of the horizontal.

Take a look at the photo of the three stones in Figure 1.12. It may not be a particularly exciting picture, but as far as balance goes, it rocks! If you were to use a piece of paper to cover any one of the three stones below, the entire photograph would feel unbalanced and unfinished. This is generally the way balance works. It's as if the entire composition is in a picture frame hanging by a single nail on the wall. It doesn't take much weight on one side or the other to shift the entire picture off balance.

Unlike symmetrical balance, asymmetrical balance is very versatile, and as such, it's used much more often on the web. If you take a look at most two-column web site layouts, you'll notice that the larger column is often very light in color—a tactic that creates a good contrast for the text and the main content. The diminutive navigational column is often darker, has some sort of border, or is made to stand out in some other way, in order to create balance within the layout. John Hicks's site, Hicksdesign, which is shown in Figure 1.13, is an excellent example of asymmetrical balance.[8] The heavy brown sidebar, which contains the logo and main navigation for the site, stays fixed on the right-hand side of the layout even when the content scrolls. This ever-present element provides interest and balance to the rest of the content on the page.

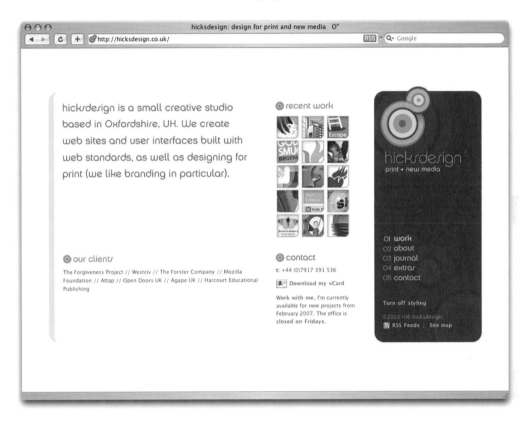

Figure 1.13: Hicksdesign—an example of asymmetrical balance

Many principles are at work in the design of John Hicks's site—this design isn't just about asymmetrical balance. The site has great harmony, which comes from the repeated, brightly colored bullets, similarly colored headers, and consistent typefaces. Part of that harmony arises from the fact that the site meets the principles of unity.

---

8   http://www.hicksdesign.co.uk/

Unity

Design theory describes **unity** as referring to the way in which the different elements of a composition interact with one another. A unified layout is one that works as a whole rather than being identified as separate pieces. Take the monkeys in Figure 1.14, for example. Their similar colors and shapes mean that they can easily be recognized as forming a group, rather than merely being four monkeys.

Figure 1.14: Unity among the monkeys

Although it's not such an issue these days, unity is one of the many reasons why web designers have always despised HTML frames. It's important that unity exists not only within each element of a web page, but across the entire web page—the page itself must work as a unit. We can use a couple of approaches to achieve unity in a layout (aside from avoiding frames): proximity and repetition.

Proximity

Proximity is an obvious, but often overlooked way to make a group of objects feel like a single unit. Placing objects close together within a layout creates a focal point toward which the eye will gravitate. Take a look at the digital painting in Figure 1.15. While composed of a seemingly random assortment of strokes, the five strokes that are the closest together appear to form a unified object.

Figure 1.15: Creating a group using proximity

We practice the concept of proximity on the Web when we start setting margins and padding for elements. For instance, when I define the CSS style rules for most sites, I usually change the default margin that exists between common HTML elements such as headings (**h1**, **h2**, **h3** …), paragraphs, blockquotes, and even images. By altering these values, I can cause more or less space to appear between elements, thereby creating groups.

If you look at the two columns of text in Figure 1.16, you'll notice that they look very similar. The only difference is in the placement of the headings. In the column on the left, the word "Unkgnome" is equi-distant from the top and bottom paragraphs. This results in a heading that looks more like a separator than a heading for the next paragraph. In the second column, the "Gnomenclature" heading is placed closer to the paragraph that follows it. In accordance with the rules of proximity, this heading appears to belong to that block of text.

Figure 1.16: Proximity between headers and content

Repetition

A gaggle of geese, a school of fish, a pride of lions. Any time you bring a set of like items together, they form a group. In the same way, repetition of colors, shapes, textures, or similar objects helps to tie a web page design together so that it feels like a cohesive unit. The example in Figure 1.17 illustrates repetition. Even though there are other similar strokes around, the nine red strokes on the left-hand side appear to be a unified group because they repeat a shape, color, and texture. The strokes to the right of this group have no repeated pattern, so they appear isolated even though there are other shapes nearby.

Figure 1.17: Creating a group using repetition

Whether you notice it or not, repetition is often used in web site designs to unify elements of the layout. A good example of this concept at work among unmodified HTML elements is the bulleted list. The bullet that precedes each list item is a visual indicator that the bullet items are parts of a whole. Repeated patterns and textures can also help to unify a design. Take a look at the screenshot of Left Justified, the personal site of Australian designer Andrew Krespanis.[9] This layout contains many eye-catching elements, but the repeated use of the red wood texture in the header, menu, and page borders literally hold this design together.

Figure 1.18: Left Justified homepage

Emphasis

Closely related to the idea of unity is the concept of emphasis or dominance. Rather than focusing on getting the various elements of a design to fit together, emphasis is about making a particular element draw the viewer's attention. When you design a web page layout, often you'll identify an item in the content, or the layout itself, that you want to stand out. Perhaps it's a button you want users to press, or an error message that you want them to read. One method of achieving such emphasis is by making that element into a focal point. A **focal point** is anything on a page that draws the viewer's eye, rather than just feeling like part of the page as a whole or blending in with its surroundings. As with unity, there are a few tried and true methods of achieving a focal point.

Placement

Although the constraints of practical web design do not often allow for it, the direct center of a composition is the point at which users look first, and is always the strongest location for producing emphasis. The further from the center an element is, the less likely it is to be noticed first; for an example of this, see Figure 1.19.

Figure 1.19: Continuance and placement—creating emphasis

Continuance

The idea behind **continuance** is that when our eyes start moving in one direction, they tend to continue along that path until a more dominant feature comes along. Figure 1.19 demonstrates this effect. Even though the bottom splotch is bigger and tends to catch your eye first, your brain can't help but go "Hey, looky there, an arrow!" You'll soon find yourself staring at the smaller object.

Continuance is also one of the most common methods that web designers use to unify a layout. By default, the left edge of headings, copy, and images placed on a web page form a vertical line down the left side of a page before any styling is applied. A simple way to expand on this concept is to use the rule of thirds to line up other page elements along the lines of your grid.

Isolation

In the same way that proximity helps us create unity in a design, isolation promotes emphasis. An item that stands out from its surroundings will tend to demand attention. Even though he's sad to not be with his buddies on the other page, the isolated monkey in Figure 1.20 stands out as a focal point on the page.

Figure 1.20: Isolation—
a sad monkey

Contrast

Contrast is defined as the juxtaposition of dissimilar graphic elements, and is the most common method used to create emphasis in a layout. The concept is simple: the greater the difference between a graphic element and its surroundings, the more that element will stand out. Contrast can be created using differences in color (which I'll discuss in more detail in Chapter 2), size, and shape. Take a look at Figure 1.21.

Figure 1.21: Woot—using orange for contrast

The site is Woot, an ecommerce web site that sells just one item per day.[10] When you look at this layout, what's the first thing that grabs your attention? My guess is it's probably the product they're selling. Products at Woot change daily, though, so what grabs your eye after that? For me, it's the **I want one!** button. Although the same colors are used elsewhere in the design, the oval shape isn't. When set against an area of white space, the button has both contrast and isolation working to emphasize it. The owners of Woot *really* want you to click that button.

Proportion

One interesting way of creating emphasis in a composition is through the use of proportion. **Proportion** is a principle of design that has to do with differences in the scale of objects. If we place an object in an environment that's of larger or smaller scale than the object itself, that object will appear larger or smaller than it does in real life. This difference in proportion draws viewers' attention to the object, as it seems out of place in that context.

---

10   http://www.woot.com/

In Figure 1.22, I've taken my monkey and superimposed him over the skyline of Manhattan to prove my point. Between the sharp contrast in color, and the difference in proportion, your brain immediately says, "Hey, something's not right here," and you're left staring at the monkey until you force yourself to look away.

Figure 1.22: Proportion—a monkey in Manhattan

This principle works for miniaturization as well. If you take a look at my personal web site, Jasongraphix, pictured in Figure 1.23, one of the first things you might notice on the page is the mini-me leaning against my artwork just under the logo.[11] As with the **I want one!** button on Woot, this little guy stands out because of contrast and isolation, but also because of the eye-catching use of proportion.

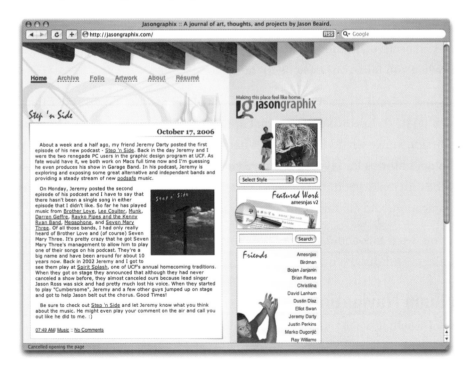

Figure 1.23: Jasongraphix—my personal site, featuring mini-me!

11   http://www.jasongraphix.com/

A few standard HTML tags and CSS properties have been designed to take advantage of the preceding theories to create emphasis in a web page even without customization. For text that is a quote, consider the **blockquote** element. This element indents the left- and right-hand side of any text placed within it, purposely breaking the continuation lines of the page content and drawing attention to itself. For positioning, consider the position property in CSS. By absolutely positioning an object with CSS, you take it out of the flow of its containing block, so you can place it strategically to draw attention. And when you think about contrast, think about the **blink** tag. Just kidding! Don't *ever* think about the **blink** tag. Yes, it creates contrast … over and over and over again. Please don't use it. Don't get any ideas about using a **marquee** tag either. Design is just as much about what we leave out as it is about what we put in.

Next, we'll look at some well-tested examples of designs from which you can work.

Bread-and-butter Layouts

Most of what we've talked about thus far has been design theory. Theory's good, but it can only take us so far toward understanding why some ideas work—and others don't—in a web site's design. In my opinion, examples and practice are much more valuable. Most academic graphic design programs include a curriculum that's rich in art history and fine art. These classes provide a great foundation for an understanding of graphic design from an art perspective, but they do little to prepare you for the specific challenges you encounter when you take your designs to the Web.

Pablo Picasso once said, "I am always doing that which I can not do, in order that I may learn how to do it." While I like to take that approach when designing a new web site, it's important first to know what you *can* do. When you look out across the Internet, you can see that the possibilities for layout really are endless. But, as I said before, only a few of those possibilities make good design sense. That's why we see certain configurations of identity, navigation, and content over and over again.

In this section, we'll talk about a few of the most common layouts, and explore some of their advantages and disadvantages.

Left-column Navigation

Regardless of whether we're talking about liquid or fixed-width layout design, the left-column navigation format is the de facto standard. The ThinkGeek site, pictured in Figure 1.24, is a classic example of this configuration.[12] Many sites that fit into this mold don't

---

12   http://www.thinkgeek.com/

necessarily use the left column as the main navigation block—sometimes you'll see the navigation along the top of the page—but they still divide the layout below the header into a narrow (one-third or less) left column and a wide right column. It's a status quo, like a security blanket, or that comfortable shirt with holes in the armpits that you wear once a week even though it drives your spouse crazy. For those reasons, a layout featuring left-column navigation is a safe choice for any project.

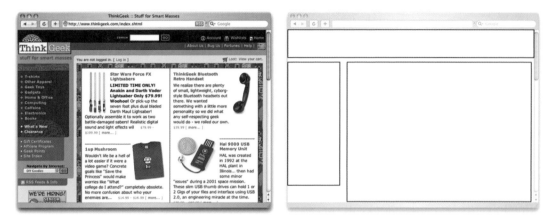

Figure 1.24: Left-column navigation at ThinkGeek

The downside to sites that use left-column navigation is that they can lack creativity. They've been done so many times, and in so many ways, that they tend to look the same. That's not to say you shouldn't use a left-column navigation layout. I'd guess that 75% of the sites I've designed have been based on the left-column navigation model, but I try to do something different when I can.

Speaking of different, how about picking that left column up and sticking it on the other side of the content? Then you'd have a right-column navigation layout.

Right-column Navigation

Although it's difficult to find sites like Audi's (depicted in Figure 1.25) that place the main site navigation along the right-hand side of the layout, it's quite easy to find sites that use a right-hand column for sub-navigation, advertising, or sub-content.[13] Since, in western cultures, our eyes scan from left to right, this allows the page's main content to be the first thing viewers see.

---

13   http://www.audi.com/

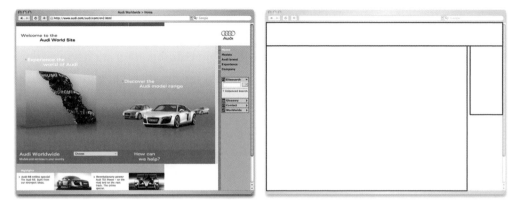

Figure 1.25: Right-column navigation on Audi's web site

I'm not sure why there aren't more sites that make use of the right column. The studies I've seen tend to swing both ways in regards to the usability and practicality of right-hand menus. In my own experience, my cursor tends to hover on the right side of the browser window anyway—so I can be closer to the scrollbar.

Ultimately, this is a judgement call that's really about the needs of your clients and how they want people to perceive their online presence. Left-column navigation is familiar and more standard, but that's not always the number one priority in designing a new site. One thing's for sure, though: if you want your design to be different from the average web site, but you still want users to be able to find your navigation, you should give a right-column layout a try.

Three-column Navigation

The typical three-column layout has a wide center column flanked by two diminutive navigational columns. The Apple Store web site shown in Figure 1.26 is an example of this common web page layout staple.[14] Although three columns may be necessary on pages that have a ton of navigation, short bits of content, or advertising to display, it's important to remember that whitespace is essential if we are to keep a layout from appearing cluttered. Fortunately at the Apple Store, the three columns only exist on the homepage, and the center column has some whitespace that helps to promote eye movement.

---

14   http://store.apple.com/

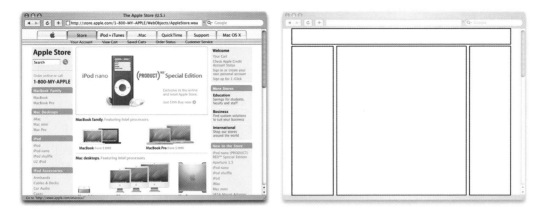

Figure 1.26: Three-column navigation at Apple Store

Getting Inspired

Just because the left-, right-, and three-column layout configurations are the bread and butter of most web page designs doesn't mean you have to be confined to these layouts. A plethora—yes, a plethora—of design showcase and gallery sites have been created to feature new and innovative ideas that might help you think outside the box, including the following (just to name a few):

- **CSS Zen Garden at http://www.csszengarden.com/**

  This site is the original showcase of fresh ideas for CSS. Even if you don't intend to design a CSS Zen Garden template, it's a great source of inspiration.

- **CSS Beauty at http://www.cssbeauty.com/**

  CSS Beauty is both a gallery of well-designed CSS web sites and a portal to the CSS design community.

- **Stylegala Gallery at http://www.stylegala.com/archive/**

  Stylegala is a great source of information about web design and standards, but the gallery features only the best-of-the-best new CSS designs.

- **CSS Vault at http://cssvault.com/**

  The CSS Vault's gallery archive goes back to November 2003, so it's not only a great source of inspiration, but a historical repository of great CSS design.

- **Design Interact Site of the Week at http://www.designinteract.com/sow/**

  Just for good measure, here's one gallery that doesn't concentrate on CSS-based designs. Design Interact is the multimedia- and technology-focused spin-off of Communication Arts, a leading trade journal for visual communication and graphic design. Design Interact has been highlighting (and archiving) a new and unique web site every week since January 1998.

Using a Morgue File

I know what you're thinking: "Great, I've got a bunch of galleries to look at, now what?" One of the most useful "tings" my first graphic design professor taught me was to create a **morgue file** whenever I worked on a large project. The concept is pretty simple: if you're doing an illustration or marketing project that involves trains, you clip out and print up anything you can find that might give you inspiration and keep it all in a folder. It helps with your current project, and should you ever need to do another project involving trains, you'll have lots of inspiration on hand.

> **NOTE   Don't have Photoshop Handy?**
>
> If you're working on a computer that doesn't have graphics editing software, keep in mind that some other common programs like Microsoft Word allow you to paste image from the clipboard into documents as well.

The morgue file idea kind of slipped my mind until a few years ago when I was working on a web site layout. I found myself looking for a similar layout to the one I wanted to create—in particular, I wanted to see how other designers handled the background textures for such a design. That was when I decided to start my digital morgue file. I started taking screenshots of sites I saw in some of the galleries listed above, and sorted them into folders with names such as leftnav, rightnav, 3column, and oddball. Having a repository of web site designs that I can look at any time has been a handy resource on countless occasions when I've been looking for inspiration.

> **TIP   Capture a Screenshot for your own Morgue File**
>
> 1. Select the browser window that's displaying the page of which you wish to save a screenshot.
> 2. Copy a screenshot of the browser window to your clipboard:
>   - On a PC, press *Alt Print Screen*.
>   - On a Mac, press *Shift Command 4*, then *Space* to turn the cursor into a camera. Then, hold down *Ctrl*, and click on the browser window.
> 3. At this point, you should have a screenshot of the browser window in your clipboard. Open a new document in your favorite graphics program and paste the screenshot.
> 4. Save your image or document.

Fresh Trends

If you're feeling so overwhelmed by the above resources that you can't even contemplate starting a morgue file for inspiration, just take a few minutes to browse through those sites. Look past the colors and textures to the boxes that make up the layout, and try to identify common ideas and design trends. By doing this, I've started to notice a few trends that seem to be emerging in web site layouts.

Expansive Footer Navigation

If you scroll to the bottoms of pages on many of the most recently redesigned sites, you're likely to see an interesting new trend. Rather than using the footer for main links and a copyright notice, many sites are expanding this neglected piece of page real estate to include contact information, expanded site navigation, and extra content such as blogrolls, linkrolls, Flickr badges, and so on. Although putting a site's main navigational element at the bottom of the page isn't a good idea, the concept of including "bonus" navigation and content in that space has taken off lately. As Figure 1.27 shows, JeffCroft.com is just one of the sites trying this approach.[15]

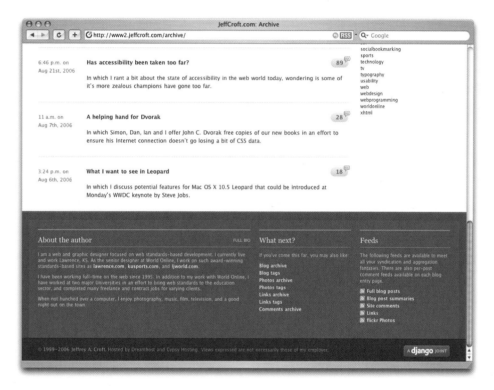

Figure 1.27: Presenting extra content in the footer at JeffCroft.com

See also:

- City Church, at http://www.thecity.org/
- Powazek, at http://www.powazek.com/
- Fresh Branding, at http://www.freshbranding.co.uk/

Three Columns with Content First

The majority of fresh three-column site designs that have been produced lately have put the content first. By first, I mean they're locating the content on the far left of the display.

---

15   http://jeffcroft.com/

As you can see in Figure 1.28, this approach produces a very modern and professional look for Vivabit.[16]

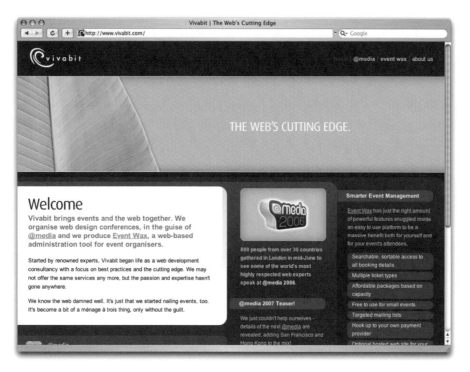

Figure 1.28: Putting content first at Vivabit.com

Although this isn't really a new idea, it's been picking up a lot of steam lately in both liquid- and fixed-width site designs. The majority of three-column layouts usually switch to a two-column structure outside the homepage. By placing the content on the left, the transition from three columns to two is more natural, as the content column can simply expand, rather than having to relocate completely. For example, if you visit any of the other main pages of the Vivabit site, the width of the content area seems simply to expand up and to the right when you navigate from the homepage into the site.

See also:

- Veerle's Blog, at http://veerle.duoh.com/
- Django, at http://www.djangoproject.com/

Resizing: Fixed Width vs. Liquid Width

Back when we were drawing layout blocks with pencil and paper, I explained that the first page element we had to think about was the containing block, and whether or not it would expand to fill the page. This decision is one that has plagued web designers for hundreds,

---

16   http://www.vivabit.com/

if not thousands of years—all the way back to the days when we used tables and *spacer.gif* files to layout web page content. Okay, maybe that wasn't actually *thousands* of years ago, but this is a long-standing debate nonetheless. In fact, the fixed-versus-liquid debate caused quite a bit of commotion back in December 2003 when two very influential designers, Douglas Bowman of Stopdesign[17] and Dan Cederholm of SimpleBits,[18] simultaneously switched from liquid- to fixed-width layouts. This caused instant and unwarranted panic among the design and web standards community, whose members feared that this move marked the death of liquid layouts.

Since then, most designers have established their own opinions in regard to the fixed-versus-liquid debate. The decision to use one type of layout over the other should really be determined by the target audience and the accessibility goals of each individual web site. The pros and cons of each layout type are fairly well-defined, as Table 1.1 illustrates.

Table 1.1: Fixed- vs. liquid-width layouts—the pros and cons

	Pros	Cons
Fixed-width	■ designer has more control over how an image floated within the content will look ■ allows for planned whitespace ■ narrower text blocks improve readability	■ can appear dwarfed in large browser windows ■ takes control away from the user
Liquid-width	■ adapts to most screen resolutions and devices ■ reduces user scrolling	■ text spanning a wide distance is more difficult to read ■ more difficult to execute successfully ■ can cause a lack of, or awkward, whitespace

With these pros and cons in mind, I've designed more fixed-width layouts than liquid. I like having control over how the content will display, and working with the background space. On the flip side, I sometimes enjoy the challenges that liquid layouts bring to the table. But, regardless of personal preferences, it's important to put the needs of your client first. If you're deciding on the width of a fixed-width layout, you have to think about the audience for which you're designing, and create a layout that meets the needs of those users.

An Alternative: Variable Fixed–width Layout

The somewhat ironic term **variable fixed-width layout** was coined by Richard Rutter in an article that he wrote to catalog his findings about this new trend.[19] It's an excellent discussion of the topic that provides some great examples.

---

17 http://stopdesign.com/
18 http://simplebits.com/
19 http://clagnut.com/blog/1663/

The homepage of Simon Collison's Colly Logic exhibits the best implementation I've seen of this new trend.[20] When you expand your browser window from 800 pixels to 1024 pixels in width, the right-hand column splits into a third column. Figure 1.29 shows how it works.

Figure 1.29: Viewing Colly Logic at 800 and 1024 pixel widths

Colly Logic acts as an intermediary between fixed- and liquid-width design. A handful of designers have been toying with this idea; CSS Beauty, one of the CSS gallery sites I mentioned earlier, takes a variable fixed-width approach to displaying features and advertising content.[21]

Screen Resolution

In comparison to the fixed-versus-liquid debate, the arguments about designing for particular screen resolutions are much more tame. When designers say that a site is designed, or optimized, for a particular screen resolution, they're actually talking about the resolution of the viewer's monitor. The debate has centered around whether or not we should design sites in such a way that people using a monitor resolution of 800×600 pixels could see the entire width of the content area with their browsers in full-screen mode. Given that we must account for sidebars and browser borders, this approach would see us design a content area that's approximately (or that could be resized to approximately) 750 pixels wide.

NOTE Screen Resolution

According to W3Schools' screen resolution statistics, in July 2006, 17% of web users had their screens set to 800×600 pixels (down from 25% in July 2005), 58% had their resolutions set at 1024×768 pixels (up from 55%), and 19% had their screens set to a resolution higher than 1024×768 pixels (up from 14%). 6% of users had their monitors set to an unknown resolution.[22] Figure 1.30 illustrates these trends.

---

20 http://www.collylogic.com/
21 http://www.cssbeauty.com/
22 http://www.w3schools.com/browsers/browsers_stats.asp

As of July, 2006, W3Schools' screen resolution statistics showed that the number of W3Schools users who set their screen resolutions to 800×600 pixels had dropped, but not to the point that it could be safely ignored—see Figure 1.30.[23]

At the time, this resolution still accounted for 17% of users, but that number had dropped by 3-5% every six months for the previous two years. Does this mean that as soon as those displays set to 800×600 have been replaced, we can all start to design sites that are 1024 pixels wide? Hardly. Even if everyone was using a resolution of 1024×768 pixels or more, not everyone will use your site with the browser window maximized.

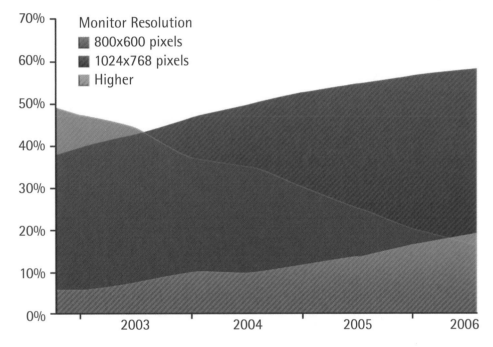

Figure 1.30: W3Schools' screen resolution statistics

Although statistics like those provided by W3Schools help to give us reason to design for higher resolutions, the most important factor in web design is the end user. If the web site you're building is for web professionals and people who are likely to use the latest computer equipment and high resolutions, it may be safe to push the design envelope and create designs that are wider than 800 pixels. The goal, though, is to prevent users from needing to scroll from left to right in order to read content. So, even if you decide to design beyond the 800-pixel standard, do not alienate the few 800×600 users you have by forcing them constantly to scroll from left to right and back again just to read your site's content. You'll only make them sea-sick!

---

23   Here, we're using W3Schools' audience as a representative sample. The statistics provide a reasonable indicator of what we could expect to find among the broader web user audience, but your target audience may have different screen resolution settings.

The August 2005 redesign of design web site A List Apart provides a great example of how a design that's wider than 800 pixels can remain accessible to users with 800×600-pixel displays.[24] Even though a horizontal scrollbar displays on the site at an 800×600 resolution, you can see all of the real content without scrolling. At 1024×768 pixels, the horizontal scrollbar disappears, and another column becomes visible on the right, displaying search functionality, topic links, and advertising. This extra column adds functionality and structure to the design of the site, but doesn't always need to be visible.

Application: Florida Country Tile

As I explained briefly in the section called "The Design Process," much of what I do when I design a new web site or print item is subconscious. I can usually tell you on a choice-by-choice basis why I made specific decisions, but it doesn't come naturally to verbalize the procedures I follow. So, for me to explain how I applied graphic design principles to create a layout for a new web site, for example, is a little difficult unless I have an example to help me break the process into steps.

Enter: Florida Country Tile, a real company and a real client. Florida Country Tile is a small, Florida-based tile and stone installation company whose owners have agreed to let me use the web site design project on which I worked with them as an example here. Currently, the company doesn't have an online presence; the only real identity collateral it has is the logo you see on the business card in Figure 1.31.

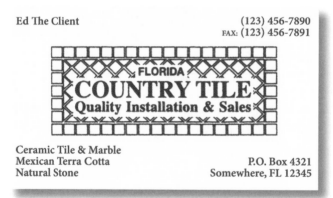

Figure 1.31: The business card of "Ed" from Florida Country Tile

I've altered the company contact information on the business card above, but that's all—other than that, this card is identical to the cards the business uses. As you can tell, this scenario isn't all that different from the one I introduced at the beginning of this chapter: the organization hasn't established a very strong visual identity.

Usually, clients have specific ideas about what the site should look like. Depending on the client, these preconceptions can either help or hinder the design process—more often, the latter. However, on this project, I've been given free rein to make all design decisions, and I plan to design the site using the principles we'll cover in each chapter of this book. Hopefully, "Ed the Client" will be happy with the results, and "You the Reader" will get a clearer picture of the design process I described so vaguely earlier in this chapter.

Getting Started

To start out, I arrange a meeting with the client to discuss his needs and desires for the web site. Unfortunately, I'm in South Carolina and Ed's in Florida, so the meeting has to take place over the phone. Even though I already know this client very well and can answer many of my own questions about his business, I call him anyway. In contrast to the approach I use on most client projects, I'll communicate with Ed about each component of the web site I'm building; I'll do so toward the end of each chapter of this book. Since this chapter is all about layout, I have three key questions to ask him:

- How much content do you want to provide on the web site?
- What kinds of content do you want to provide on the web site?
- Is the logo on the business card used consistently across all collateral to brand your company?

I want to get an idea of how many pages I'll be working with, so that I can anticipate how large my main navigation menu will be. Before I call Ed, I jot down a list of the pages I'd expect on a small web site: Home, About, and Contact. After thinking about the tile industry a bit more, and looking at other tile web sites, I decide to add Gallery, Services, and Estimate Request pages.

When I speak with Ed, he's pleased with this list of pages, but he wants to know if he could add another page or two in the future. I assure him that I'll work some flexibility into the layout to accommodate the possibility of extra pages, and explain that he can also include subpages within each of these main sections.

I also explain that the reason I want to know about the company's logo is that the current rectangular tile pattern background limits the design possibilities that are available to us. He understands this, and says that the company shirts use a simplified pattern, shown in Figure 1.32, and use only the words "Country Tile." He suggests I use that style of logo if I think it will work better.

The conversation is helpful. I obtain the information I need about the content, and it looks like I've got a little flexibility with the logo presentation. With a navigation list of only six to eight pages, I could use a side navigation bar, but I have plenty of room to place the navigation along the top of the page. In fact, that sounds pretty good to me. I think it's time to move on to a grid.

Figure 1.32: Embroidered Country Tile logo

Rather than sticking to my wide-ruled 79¢ spiral notebook, I pull a piece of blank paper out of my printer tray and draw out four 3×3 grids. I'm not sure exactly how I want to present the logo. That doesn't matter at this point, though—I'm just trying to decide how to configure my blocks. After all that talk about how right-column layouts don't get a lot of use, I'm thinking about having a multi-purpose sidebar on the right-hand side of the display. I can see us using this area for content on some pages, for a gallery or featured item on the homepage, and possibly as a subnavigation section on the Services page. I can use the emphasis properties we talked about earlier to make the content section stand out, but I'll keep in mind our discussion of unity to make sure that this sub-column fits into the overall page design.

With those parameters in mind, I quickly sketch out the four ideas depicted in Figure 1.33.

In the first sketch (upper-left), the sidebar and main content are top-aligned within the upper third of the square. It looks okay, but is fairly basic.

For my second attempt (upper-right), I went with a left- instead of a right-hand column. I then put the logo over the content and added an image of a company van above the sidebar. Immediately, I decided that I didn't like this logo placement—I thought the left-hand column was getting too much emphasis. Plus, the van looked like the Mystery Mobile— "Like, Zoinks!!"

My third attempt (lower-left) wasn't much better. I started off by putting the logo in the bottom of the upper-left square of my grid, and although I liked the location of the content area, the blocky business card logo presentation stopped the layout from looking unified.

Time for a fourth attempt (lower-right), with one ball and two strikes (to borrow from Baseball parlance). For the content and sidebar areas, I decided to use shapes that were similar to my third sketch, but I placed the logo and menu as close as possible to the top of the layout. Then, I realized that I could use the area between the top of the content and the navigation bar as an image gallery.

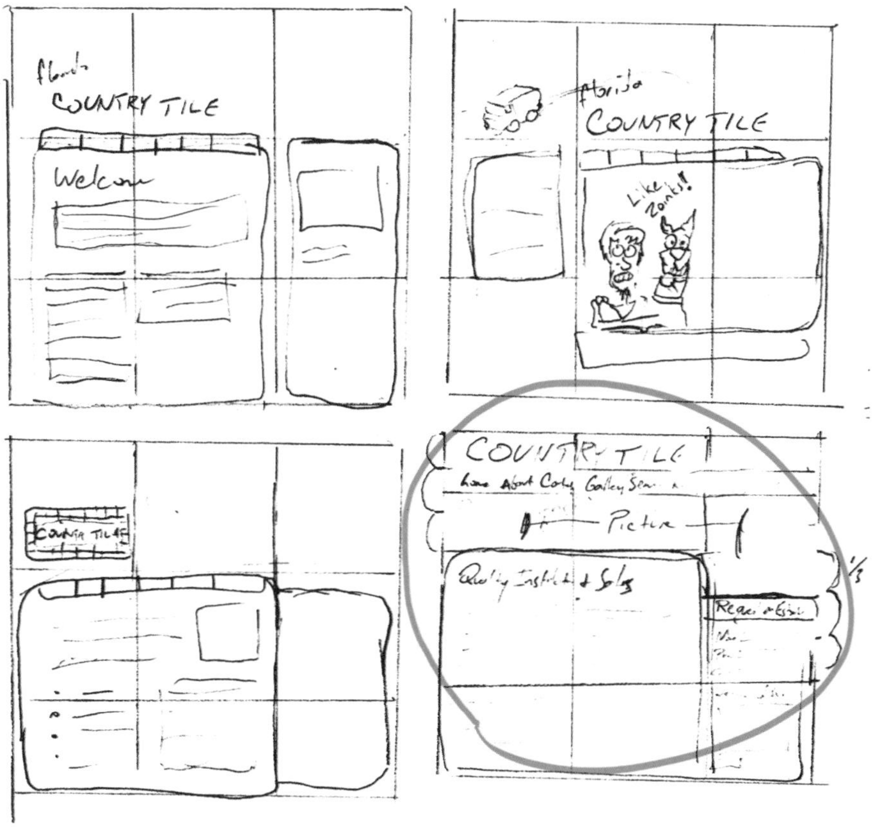

Figure 1.33: 3×3 grid sketches for Florida Country Tile—please ignore the Mystery Mobile

I'm quite pleased with the final sketch, so I choose it instead of the first one, and decide to move on to build the layout using gray boxes in Adobe Illustrator. I don't anticipate having a lot of content for this site, so I think it would be best to restrict it to a fixed-width design. Whenever I know I'm dealing with a fixed-width site, my mind always jumps to the question of what we'll see outside the boundaries of the containing block. Will that block blend with the background, or will a different color or background pattern display there? We'll discuss those choices in detail in later chapters.

I start out in the graphics program the same way I started on paper. I create my 3×3 grid and work within it to create a layout that's similar to the one I scratched out on paper. Even though I used a few shades of gray, I'm not worried about choosing colors yet—that's what the next chapter's going to be about. At the moment, I'm just trying to create contrast between the blocks so that I can tell what's what, and where I intend to use separate colors. Figure 1.34 shows the results of my handiwork.

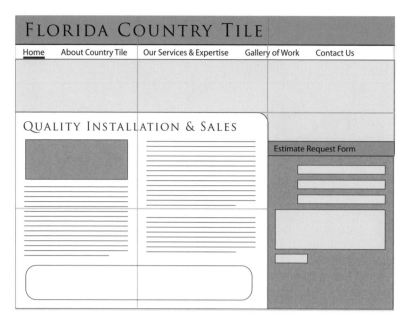

Figure 1.34: Initial gray box layout for Florida Country Tile

Earlier in the chapter, I said that in a good design, users "recognize each page as belonging to the design." That doesn't necessarily mean that the layout of each page has to be exactly the same. In fact, I usually try to work in some contrast between the homepage and the rest of the site. Right now, I'm just trying to get the general layout nailed down. Once I've defined my layout, and I've given it some color and texture, I'll modify that layout so that the homepage has a little more of a graphical feel. To get an idea of what I mean, take a look at Figure 1.35, which shows the homepage and the Zen Stories page from Roan Lavery's personal site, Renegade Zen.[25]

Notice how Roan has expanded the header area on the homepage to include some introductory content. Also, check out the changes in the content areas between these two pages. On the homepage, the first thing we see are pictures and graphics—three columns of them. In contrast, the Zen Stories section, which features text only, has been reduced to two columns. The design has consistency even though the layouts have been modified slightly to serve the specific purposes of the different pages. This is the kind of contrast I was talking about earlier, and these are the kinds of layout changes I'd eventually like to make in the Florida Country Tile layout. For now though, I have a solid base layout. It's time to move on to the next subject: color!

25 http://renegadezen.com/

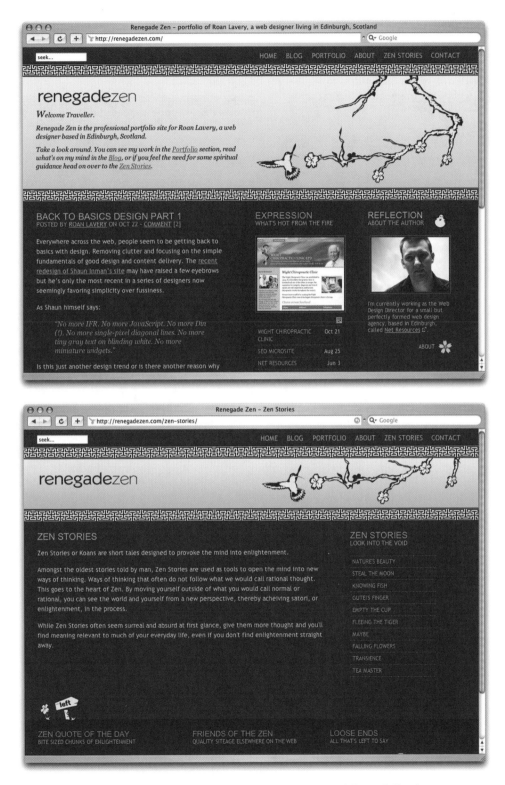

Figure 1.35: Homepage and Zen Stories page from Roan Lavery's Renegade Zen site

CHAPTER 2

Color

Whether you're defusing a ticking time bomb, or you're trying to design a decent-looking site, if you choose the wrong color, you're doomed. Okay, so the wrong color selection for a client's site might not be the death of you, but it could curtail your budding career as a web designer.

Choosing colors is no simple matter. There are aesthetic, identity, and usability considerations to take into account. And, to make matters worse, most modern displays can render more than 16 million colors. That's an infinite number of horrible color combinations just waiting to happen!

Fortunately, you don't have to be a swatchbook-carrying color consultant to make good color choices. A wealth of knowledge is available, from touchy-feely (as I like to call them) psychological guidelines to tried-and-true color theories that will help you to make the right choices when it comes to color.

The Psychology of Color

Color psychology is a field of study that's devoted to analyzing the emotional and behavioral effects produced by colors and color combinations. Ecommerce web site owners want to know which color will make their web site visitors spend more money. Home decorators want to know which color will transform a bedroom into a tranquil Zen retreat. Fast food restaurant owners are dying to know which color combinations will make you want to super-size your meal. As you can imagine, color psychology is big business.

Although it's important to know how your color choices might affect the masses, the idea that there is a single, unified, psychological response to specific colors is spurious. Many of the responses that color psychologists accredit to certain colors are rooted in individual experience. It's also interesting to note that many cultures have completely different associations with, and interpretations of, colors. With those caveats in mind, let's explore some general psychological associations that the majority of people in Western culture have in response to specific colors.

Color Associations

Describing the emotional connections that people may have with colors can be a very "hippy-esque" topic. If you don't believe me, just head over to your favorite online music store and sample some tracks from *Colors* by Ken Nordine. Although most designers don't rely solely on the supposed meanings, characteristics, and personalities of specific colors, it's still handy to have an understanding of the emotional attributes of some of the main color groups.

■ **red**

The color red has a reputation for stimulating adrenaline and blood pressure. Along with those physiological effects, red is also known to increase human metabolism. It is an exciting, dramatic, and rich color; after all, red is also a color of passion. Nothing says "love" like painting a wall bright red on Saint Valentine's Day for your sweetheart, as someone's done in Figure 2.1. The darker shades of red, such as burgundy and maroon, have a rich, indulgent feeling about them—in fact, they can be quite hoity-toity. Think about these colors when designing anything for wine enthusiasts or connoisseurs of fine living. The more earthy, brownish shades of red are associated with the fall season and harvest.

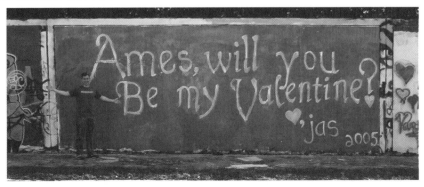

Figure 2.1: Red, the color of passion (two gallons of it!)

orange

Like red, orange is a very active and energetic color, though it doesn't evoke the anger that red sometimes does. Instead, orange is thought to promote happiness and represents sunshine, enthusiasm, and creativity. Orange is a more informal and less corporate-feeling color, which is perhaps the reason the marketing gurus behind companies such as Cingular in the US and Orange in Europe decided to create brands with it. Since orange also stimulates metabolism and appetite, it's a great color for promoting food and cooking. That's probably why the picture of a tangerine in Figure 2.2 is making you hungry, even if you don't like citrus fruits.

Figure 2.2: Orange you glad I didn't say banana?

yellow

Yellow is a highly active and visible color, which is why it's used for taxicabs and caution signs. It's associated with happiness and energy, and, as Figure 2.3 illustrates, is the signature color of smileys. Like red and orange, pure yellow is a visibly active color. The original orange and lemon-lime flavors of the sports energy drink Gatorade are still the best-selling of the brand's products. This is likely due, in part at least, to the active, energetic characteristics associated with the colors orange and yellow. An anonymous quote that's often used with color associations says, "Babies cry more in yellow rooms, husbands and wives fight more in yellow kitchens, and opera singers throw more tantrums in yellow dressing rooms." Whether this comment is true or not, the point is that too much yellow can be overpowering. Come on—if you were a baby stuck in a dressing room with fighting spouses and tantrum-throwing opera singers, you'd cry too!

Figure 2.3: Yellow, the color of smileys

green

Green is associated with nature. It is a very soothing color that symbolizes growth, freshness, and hope. It's much easier on the eyes, and far less active, than yellow, orange, or red. Although many web site designs that use green appeal to visitors' sense of nature, green is a very versatile color. When bright green is set against a black background, it really pops, and gives the design a techy feel. For me, it brings back memories of my first computer, a trusty old Apple IIe, the display of which is shown in Figure 2.4.

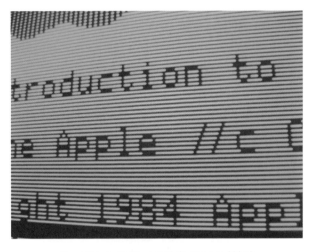

Figure 2.4: Apple IIe—a study in green and black

blue

When I was a kid, my favorite color was blue. Not just any blue, but Crayola Crayon *cerulean* blue, shown in Figure 2.5. Yeah, I was a weird kid. On the touchy-feely level, blue symbolizes openness, intelligence, and faith. Physiologically, blue has been found to calm people down, but it can also reduce appetite. This effect is probably due in part to the rarity of blue in real food. Aside from blueberries, how many naturally blue foods can you count? Blue, it would seem, is just not a part of Nature's appetite-inducing palette, so it's not a great choice for promoting food products. Blue is sometimes seen as a symbol of bad luck and trouble. This emotional color connection is evident in blues music and in the paintings of Picasso's depression-induced Blue Period. It's not all about unnatural food colors and downtrodden forms of art, though—blue also has universal appeal because of its association with the sky and the sea. This visual connection with water, sky, and air makes blue an obvious choice for web sites associated with airlines, air conditioning, pool filters, and cruises. Have you ever noticed that blue is the primary color in the logos of IBM, Dell, HP, and Microsoft? The reason for this is that blue also conveys a sense of stability and clarity of purpose ... that is, until you've experienced the blue screen of death!

Figure 2.5: There's just nothing like cerulean

purple

Historically, the color purple has been associated with royalty and power. The secret behind purple's prestigious past has to do with the difficulty of producing the dye needed to create purple garments. To this day, purple still represents wealth and extravagance. That extravagance is carried over into nature. Purple is most often connected with flowers, gemstones, and sunsets, which, when you consider Figure 2.6, is really no wonder. If you're trying to create a web site design that stands out from the crowd, think about using a rich shade of purple. According to CSS Zen Garden's Design category index, purple is by far the least commonly used color.[1]

Figure 2.6: Birds flying in front of a purple sunset

---

1   http://www.mezzoblue.com/zengarden/alldesigns/categories/

■ **white**

When people think "clean," they think of white. White is considered to be the color of perfection, light, and purity. This is why crisp white sheets are used in detergent commercials and why a bride wears a white dress on her wedding day. We often overlook these associations because of the default use of white as a background color, but they persist nonetheless. To get an idea of how ingrained the meaning of white is in our culture, just read the poem *Design* by Robert Frost. In it, Frost symbolically contradicts those associations by using white to represent death and darkness. Using colors in unexpected ways can be a good way to make a bold statement.

■ **black**

Although black often has negative connotations such as death and evil, it can also be a color of power, elegance, and strength, depending on how it's used. If you're considering using a particular color and are wondering what the associations are for that color, just ask yourself, "What are the first three things that come to mind when I think about this color?" When I think about black, for instance, I think about Johnny Cash, tuxedos, and Batman. When I think about Johnny Cash, his dark clothing, deep voice, and sorrowful songs give a tangible meaning to the mental associations I perceive between the man and the color. If you analyze your top three color associations this way, you're bound to hit some common chords that other people share in regards to your color choices.

Figure 2.7: Black, a color that represents power, elegance, and in this case, exorbitance

Even though color psychology does play a role in the way a visitor may see a site that you design, keep in mind that there is no *wrong* color to use. While psychological reasoning may help get your palette started, the success of a color scheme depends on the harmony that exists between all the colors chosen. To achieve this harmony, we'll need to keep a few other attributes of color in mind.

Color Temperature

One attribute of color that exists across the entire spectrum is the notion of color temperature. Which color faucet gives you hot water? What color do you associate with ice? Why? The answers are obvious, and are enforced by both culture and nature.

Warm Colors

Warm colors are the colors from red to yellow, including orange, pink, brown, and burgundy. Due to their association with the sun and fire, warm colors represent both heat and motion. When placed near a cool color, a warm color will tend to pop out, dominate, and produce the visual emphasis that we talked about in Chapter 1.

Cool Colors

Cool colors are the colors from green to blue, and can include some shades of violet. Violet is the intermediary between red and blue, so a cooler violet is, as you probably guessed, one that's closer to blue, while a more red violet can feel very warm. Cool colors can calm people down and reduce tension. In a design, cool colors tend to recede, making them great for backgrounds and larger elements on a page, since they won't overpower your content.

Color Value

The measure of the lightness or darkness of a color is known as its **value**. The use of light and dark colors helps to establish the classic dichotomy of good versus evil. When you think about your favorite fictional villains and heroes, what colors come to mind? In one corner we have Dr. Evil, Freddy Krueger, and the Wicked Witch of the West. In the other corner we have Luke Skywalker, Gandalf the White, and William Wallace. If you had to come up with colored jerseys for each of these improbable teams, where would you start?

If you wanted to accentuate the lightness of the good guys, you'd start off either with a pure color, such as blue, or a lighter **tint** of another cool color. A tint is made by adding white to a given color, and tints of color tend to look soft and ethereal. Even lighter shades of warm colors tend to have a fairy tale quality. Our good guys aren't softies, though, so we wouldn't want to go too light and make them look like pastel Easter ornaments.

On the other hand, dark colors feel heavy and dense. The bad guys on our opposing team all look good in black, but that might be a little too stereotypical for this motley crew. If we wanted to assign them a color, we'd probably use a dark **shade** of a warm color. A shade is any pure color to which black has been added. A nice dark red would give these guys a significant level of evil authority, don't you think?

Figure 2.8: Color value at work

Saturation

The **saturation** or **intensity** of a color is described as the brightness or dullness of that color. It's obvious that intense, vivid colors stand out. Even though cool colors tend to recede, a vivid blue will draw more attention to itself than a creamy, dull orange. I started to touch on this point above, when I said that we shouldn't make our heroes' jerseys too light. When we add gray (black *and* white) to a color, it starts to become dull and desaturated. Like cloudy water in a swimming pool, or an overcast winter morning, these colors just aren't as visually exciting or appealing as bright, vivid colors. On the bright side—no pun intended—dull colors help to reduce tension and give compositions a meditative, dreamy mood.

Figure 2.9: Value and saturation

Color Theory 101

To take our foundational knowledge of color any further, we'll need to get a grounding in some of the more technical concepts associated with the subject, such as how colors are formed and how they can be categorized.

The colors displayed on computer screens (i.e. the colors we'll be using in our web site designs) are based on an **additive color model**. In an additive color model, colors are displayed in percentages of red, green, and blue (**RGB**) light. If we turn all three of these colors on full blast, we get white light. If we turn red and green all the way up, but switch off blue, we get yellow.

If you've ever owned a color printer, you might be familiar with the acronym **CMYK** (cyan, magenta, yellow, and black). Your inkjet printer, laser printer, and industrial four-color printing press all create images using cyan, magenta, yellow, and black inks or toners. This process uses a **subtractive color model**. By combining colors together in a subtractive color model, we get closer to grayish black. You can't get black from just cyan, magenta, and yellow. You have to have black ink, which is where the K comes in. Take a look at Figure 2.10 to get a better idea of how additive and subtractive color models work.

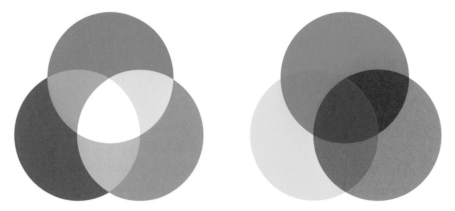

Figure 2.10: The RGB additive color model (left) and the CMYK subtractive color model (right)

Regardless of whether you're designing for print or the Web, the lessons of traditional color theory are the keys that help us classify colors and group them together. Recorded studies of color classification date back to the third century BC and the works of Aristotle. Since then, many other great artists and philosophers have contributed to our knowledge of how colors work, including Isaac Newton, Johann Wolfgang von Goethe, and Johannes Itten. The works of these three individuals, in the 17th, 18th, and 19th centuries respectively, provided the foundations on which much of our understanding of color lies. All three theorists explained colors in relation to a color wheel, using red, yellow, and blue as the primary colors. The **color wheel** is a simple but effective diagram developed to present the concepts and terminology of color theory. The traditional artists' color wheel is a circle divided into 12 slices, as Figure 2.11 indicates. Each slice is a primary color, a secondary color, or a tertiary color.

primary colors

The primary colors of the traditional color wheel are red, yellow, and blue. These hues form an equilateral triangle on the color wheel, and every fourth color from one primary color is another primary.

■ **secondary colors**

By mixing two neighboring primary colors, we create secondary colors, which are indicated here by the smaller gray triangles. The secondary colors are orange, green, and purple.

■ **tertiary colors**

There's a total of six tertiary colors: vermilion (red-orange), marigold (yellow-orange), chartreuse (yellow-green), aquamarine (blue-green), violet (blue-purple), and magenta (red-purple). As you might already have guessed, the tertiary colors are formed by mixing a primary color with an adjacent secondary color.

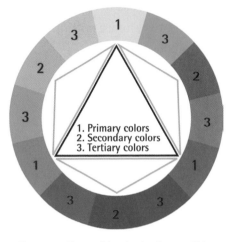

Figure 2.11: The traditional red, yellow, and blue artists' color wheel

Red, Yellow, and Blue or CMYK?

A while ago, I wrote an article for SitePoint entitled *Color for Coders*.[2] Since then, I've been amazed by the lack of respect that exists for the red, yellow, and blue primary color wheel. I've heard people call it a kindergarten tool, invalid, and archaic. It's true that the red, yellow, and blue color wheel is not a scientifically accurate model of the biological perception of light. Many people want to eliminate the red, yellow, and blue color wheel from art curricula, and establish the CMYK color wheel, shown in Figure 2.12, as the universal color model. Also, note that the secondary colors in the CMYK color wheel are red, green, and blue, meaning that we could use the CMYK model to illustrate both additive (using light) and subtractive (on paper) color.

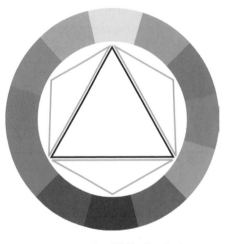

Figure 2.12: The CMYK color wheel

To illustrate the reasoning behind the push to move to CMYK, I've used gouache paints, which are basically watercolors that come in a tube. When mixed with water, they are fairly translucent and produce the colors you would expect to see on the "modern" CMYK color wheel, as Figure 2.13 shows. Magenta and yellow mix to produce nice shades of orangey reds, while cyan and yellow mix to produce green and minty tones. This is how CMYK printing works. The inks are very translucent and the overlap between them (along

---

2   http://www.sitepoint.com/article/color-for-coders/

with the use of black—don't forget good ole K) gives us most of the colors we can see on an additive, light-emitting monitor or TV. As Bob Ross might say, "that's a happy little color model."

Figure 2.13: Playing with CMY gouache paints—notice the purple

Wait! What's that purple thing? Yes, equal amounts of cyan and magenta form a violet or purple, not the pure blue suggested by the CMYK color wheel. Numerous anomalies like this crop up when we mix opaque pigments. Basically, if your paint is so thick that you can't see the white paper or canvas on which you're painting, the concepts of a CMYK color wheel start to fail. In this regard, the traditional red, yellow, and blue color wheel developed by Goethe, Itten, and many others over the last four centuries or so is a much better model.

But we're using pixels, not paint! The reason many digital artists still keep a red, yellow, and blue color wheel handy is because the color schemes and concepts of traditional color theory are based on that model. The color schemes that I covered in my SitePoint article (and which we'll discuss in the next few pages) are based on the red, yellow, and blue color model. We can't simply move the red and blue around the colour wheel and call it a day. As many of our color schemes and color combinations are based on the red, yellow, and blue color model, moving colors around the wheel would cause many problems with artistic color combinations.

There are flaws to be found in both color wheel models, and complementary colors are a prime example. But it's really going to bake your noodle when I tell you that there is no color wheel that can fully describe the complexities of the way in which we perceive color from light. Even though I design mostly for the Web—a medium that's displayed in RGB—I still use red, yellow, and blue as the basis for my color selections. I believe that color combinations created using the red, yellow, and blue color wheel are more aesthetically pleasing, and that good design is about aesthetics. Therefore, I'm going to present color theory as I learned it in my sophomore design fundamentals class at college—from the traditional red, yellow, and blue color wheel.

The Scheme of Things

Currently, we know enough about colors to talk about their values, intensities, psychological associations, temperatures, and locations on the traditional color wheel. That's all well and good, but how do we find multiple colors that work together? This is where **color schemes** come in handy. Color schemes are the basic formulae for creating harmonious and effective color combinations. Six classic color schemes exist:

- monochromatic
- analogous
- complementary
- split complementary
- triadic
- tetradic (also called double complementary)

In order to employ any of these classic color schemes, we must start with a color. Consider the subject of the web site you're working on, and choose a base color that suits the site's purpose. Of course, this choice may not always be in your hands. Sometimes, you'll have to work within a company's rules, perhaps adhering to seemingly inane and eccentric color guidelines. Let's assume that the site you're designing is for a proud family of hoity-toity circus monkeys. These circus monkeys still believe they have a royal lineage, so they have requested that we incorporate a regal purple into the design. Silly monkeys … but you know what they say: "the client is always right."

A Monochromatic Color Scheme

When we talked about the value of color earlier, we talked about tints and shades. A **monochromatic color scheme** consists of a single base color and any number of tints or shades of that color. Here's our regal monkey in Figure 2.14, where you can see a monochromatic color scheme in purple.

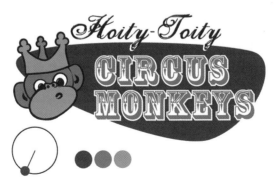

Figure 2.14: A monochromatic monkey

Monochromatic Color Scheme Examples

The promotional web site for Mint, a web site statistics tracking application developed by Shaun Inman, is as helpful as it is elegant.[3] Both the web site and the Mint application itself use a unified, mostly monochromatic color scheme comprising various shades and tints of the color green, as you can see in Figure 2.15.

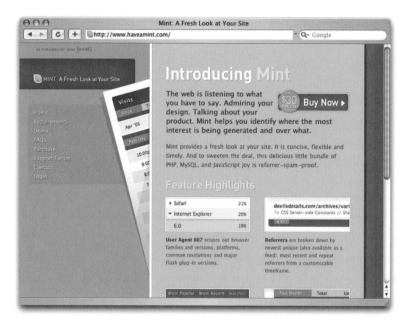

Figure 2.15: Mint web page—monochromatism in green

Figure 2.16: Blue Flavor—blue as branding

When your branding and identity efforts start with a color, a monochromatic color scheme is an obvious choice. The guys at the consulting and design firm Blue Flavor took this idea and ran with it.[4] Have a look at Figure 2.16—rather than choosing colors to suit the brand, they've taken the color blue and made it *into* their brand for a uniquely simple color scheme.

Superfluous Banter is the

---

3   http://www.haveamint.com/
4   http://www.blueflavor.com/

personal site of designer Dan Rubin.[5] In his latest web site redesign (or "reboot" as Dan likes to call it), Dan created a theme called *Orangina* that uses the color orange in a very big way. As with the previous two examples of monochromatic color schemes, this design really stands out, as you can see in Figure 2.17. We're so used to seeing multiple color designs on the Web that when a design that uses only one color comes along, it really catches us off guard—especially when that color is bright orange.

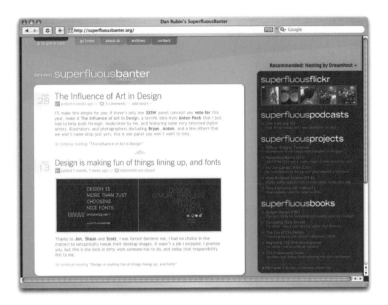

Figure 2.17: Superfluous Banter web page—a theme in orange

Although Khoi Vinh's Subtraction web site (Figure 2.18) uses orange for the hover color of links and some accent graphics,[6] his design is really an **achromatic color scheme**. The word achromatic literally means "without color," so an achromatic color scheme is one that is created using only black, white, and shades of gray. Because achromatic color schemes are merely shades and tints of gray, they're still monochromatic, though perhaps a little more special.

Figure 2.18: Subtraction web page—an achromatic color scheme

5   http://www.superfluousbanter.org/
6   http://www.subtraction.com/

Figure 2.19: An analogous monkey

An Analogous Color Scheme

An **analogous color scheme** consists of colors that are adjacent to one another on the color wheel. If our color wheel were a cheesecake, then an analogous color scheme would be a fairly large slice. The key to creating a good analogous scheme is to remember that your eyes are bigger than your appetite. As a rule of thumb, don't take a slice bigger than one-third of the whole, or you're bound to make *somebody* sick. Getting back to our hoity-toity monkeys: in the design shown in Figure 2.19, we've taken their purple and made it feel warm with some orange tones.

Analogous Color Scheme Examples

I mentioned before that orange was a good color to use to promote food and that maroons and burgundys have a very rich feeling to them. The site for Regine's Patisserie takes advantage of the psychological effects of both of those colors.[7] This delicious confection of a web site is oozing with flavor and warmth, as Figure 2.20 shows. If the colors don't kick-start your appetite, the product photography will.

Figure 2.20: Regine's Patisserie—mmm

7   http://www.regines.net.au/

Blinksale, shown in Figure 2.21, is a hosted web-application that creates, manages, and sends CSS-formatted and plain-text invoices.[8] It's also an excellent example of what a creative analogous color scheme can do for a business web site. It crumples up those preconceived notions of how corporate web sites should look, and tosses them into a cool sea of colors ranging from blue-green to yellow.

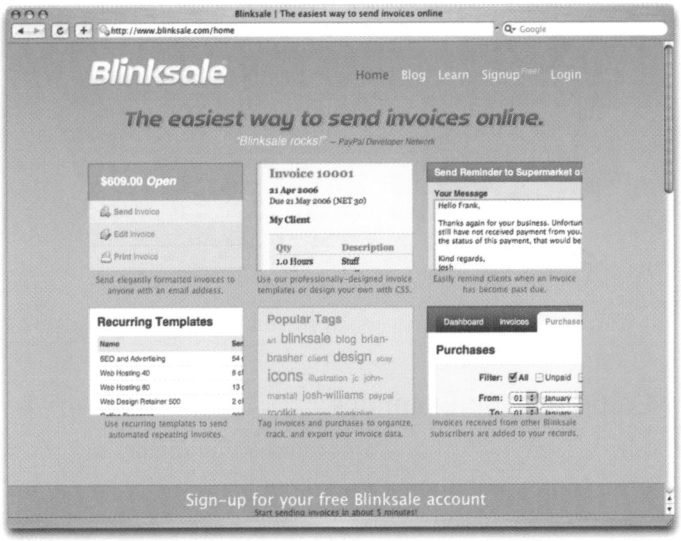

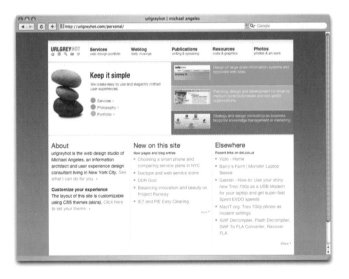

Figure 2.21: Blinksale—one cool business web site

Although the colors of Michael Angeles' urlgreyhot web site change from section to section, the color scheme of the homepage is predominantly analogous, as shown in Figure 2.22.[9]

Figure 2.22: urlgreyhot homepage—analogous and earthy

WARNING   *Changing Color Schemes*

Many web sites use different color schemes for each section of content. This approach can add richness and character to the content, but it can also produce some identity issues. If you're going to use multiple color schemes within a single site, be sure to keep the logo, menu, and overall layout of the site consistent to avoid confusion.

---

8   http://www.blinksale.com/
9   http://urlgreyhot.com/

A Complementary Color Scheme

Complementary color schemes like that illustrated in Figure 2.23 consist of colors that are located opposite each other on the color wheel, such as green and red, yellow and violet, or orange and blue. These colors are said to complement one another.

Figure 2.23: A funky complementary monkey

Complementary Color Scheme Examples

The University of Florida is my wife's undergraduate alma mater, and the school's orange and blue team colors provide a great foundation for a complementary color scheme.[10] Some people may be put off by the stark contrast of complementary color schemes illustrated in Figure 2.24, but when the colors represent the business or entity for which you're designing, you can't go wrong. The group behind the university's redesign did a great job of joining these unlikely color choices with a beautiful layout and standards-compliant markup.

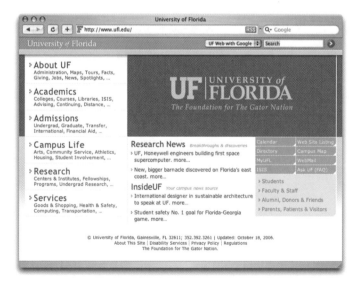

Figure 2.24: The University of Florida's home page

---

10   http://www.ufl.edu/

Faith Inkubators is an organization dedicated to designing, testing, and tweaking education resources for the growing Christian faith.[11] The violet of its logo is used throughout the site, shown in Figure 2.25, and is balanced by the use of a neutral yellow.

Figure 2.25: Faith Inkubators homepage

With a name like Rob Goodlatte, how could you go wrong with a palette of coffee tones and earthy colors? Rob is a designer and a Duke University student who seems to have a firm grasp on the principles of graphic design.[12] The use of green as a sidebar and accent color for the design shown in Figure 2.26 isn't an obvious choice, but it takes the overall design from being a simple analogous theme to a sophisticated complementary palette.

Figure 2.26: Rob Goodlatte web page—coffee and green tones

---

11   http://www.faithink.com/
12   http://www.robgoodlatte.com/

Common Complementary Pitfalls

Since complementary colors are so different from each other in so many ways, they can cause an effect known as **simultaneous contrast** when placed together: each color makes the other appear more vibrant and dominant. This effect is actually what makes complementary color schemes so successful at moving visitors' eyes around a composition. However, it can be horribly painful when complementary colors are used in a foreground–background relationship, as they are in Figure 2.27.

Figure 2.27: Simultaneous contrast

Another common pitfall is to choose colors that are not quite directly opposite one another on the color wheel, yet are not close enough to be analogous colors. These combinations are known as **discordants** because the colors will often clash with one another, causing viewers to feel discord. In fact, 1980s fashion was all about discordant colors. Seeing a discordant color scheme these days tends to bring back fond memories of that geometric "designer series" of Trapper Keeper binders I loved so dearly in middle school—one's reproduced in Figure 2.28.

Figure 2.28: A discordant Trapper Keeper cover

On that faintly positive note, this pitfall can be made workable if it's used intentionally. Discordant colors are "whiz-bang" combinations that really appeal to children, so using them for kids' sites or products isn't out of the question. They can also be used *sparingly* in more grown-up designs to create greater emphasis than can be achieved with just a simple complementary combination. Note my emphasis on the word *sparingly*, though!

Split-complementary, Triadic, and Tetradic Color Schemes

Split-complementary, triadic and tetradic color schemes sound technical, but they're really just simple variations of a basic complementary color scheme.

To create a **split-complementary** color scheme, use the two colors adjacent to your base color's complement. For example, take the left-hand color scheme shown in Figure 2.29. Red is base color here, so instead of using green to form a complementary scheme, we'll use the two colors adjacent to green, chartreuse (yellow-green) and aquamarine (blue-green), to form a three-color split complementary scheme. Note that, since you're using your base color with two discordant colors, this type of color scheme can look juvenile and extreme.

Figure 2.29: Split-complementary color scheme examples

For a **triadic** color scheme, we just push our split-complements out one more notch on each side, so that all the colors are equally spaced. Instead of selecting chartreuse (yellow-green), we select yellow, and instead of aquamarine (blue-green), we select blue. By doing this, we divide the color wheel into thirds, hence the tri- prefix in the name *tri*adic. In this example, which is the left-hand scheme in Figure 2.30, we have the three primaries (red, yellow, and blue) making up our color scheme. If you turned the scheme clockwise one notch, you'd have chartreuse (yellow-green), violet (blue-purple), and vermilion (red-orange), as shown in the middle example in Figure 2.30.

Figure 2.30: Triadic color scheme examples

Knowing that triadic color schemes involve three colors, you've probably already deducted from your extensive knowledge of the Greek language (okay, so maybe you haven't) that a **tetradic** color scheme involves four colors. A tetradic color scheme is one in which any complementary color scheme is combined with another complementary color scheme. The left-hand color scheme in Figure 2.31 is a tetradic color scheme that combines orange and blue with yellow and purple.

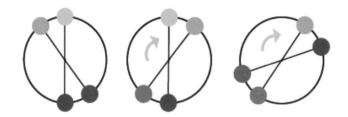

Figure 2.31: Tetradic color scheme examples

Other Variants

It's actually fairly difficult to find pure examples of the six classic color schemes I described above. Although most designers are aware of these standard color schemes, the combinations can tend to feel basic and uninspired. However, if you treat the color wheel like a dartboard, and pick whatever colors you land on, you're likely to come up with some truly awful combinations. Rather than taking that risk, there are plenty of ways to tweak the classic color schemes to create something fresh. Once you have a handle on monochromatic, analogous, and complementary color relationships, try experimenting with some of the following:

- **monochromatic with mo' pop**
  Rather than just using tints and shades of your base color, try incorporating pure gray, black, and white. This will create more contrast and more "pop" within a monochromatic color scheme.
- **analo-adjust**
  Adjust the saturation of one of the colors in your monochromatic scheme up and adjust the others down. A highly saturated color will stand out when placed among muted colors. There should be no analo-guessing which one is the saturated color.
- **mono-split-complement**
  If you've got a good thing going with a split-complement color scheme, but want to add some depth, try using a few tints and shades of your base color in the design.

Obviously, I just made those names up, but you'll notice that all three variants are very similar to the main traditional schemes. It's easy to tweak the traditional color schemes a little to get more character out of them, but remember that the color scheme you choose is the foundation from which you will build your web site's color palette. It's important to build on a firm foundation, or the rest of your design could come tumbling down.

Creating a Palette

"A palette?" you might ask. "Isn't that the same as a color scheme?" Well, yes and no. A color scheme will only give you two, three, or four colors to work with. Although a limited palette is a beautiful thing, you're probably going to need a few other colors to design your web site. It's best to get this process nailed down while you're thinking in the language of color, than to pick ancillary colors at random as you need them for your layout. The number of colors you'll need will depend on the complexity of your design. I like to start off with at least six solid color choices before I even think about going back to apply them to my layout.

Hexadecimal Notation

Since this is the stage in which we get specific about each color we're choosing, we're going to need a standard way to refer to the colors in our palette. You probably already know about hexadecimal RGB color values, but if you don't, here's the quick, drive-thru version of the theory.

The hexadecimal counting system is much like the decimal counting system you're used to, except that instead of being based on multiples of ten, the hexadecimal counting system is based on multiples of 16, and has six additional digits: A (which is the equivalent of decimal 10), B (11), C (12), D (13), E (14), and F (15). Table 2.1 shows how we count from 1 to 255 in decimal and hexadecimal.

Table 2.1: Counting from 1 to 255 in hexadecimal

Decimal	Hexadecimal	Decimal	Hexadecimal	Decimal	Hexadecimal
0	00	16	10	32	20
1	01	17	11	33	21
2	02	18	12	34	22
3	03	19	13	35	23
4	04	20	14	...	
5	05	21	15	245	F5
6	06	22	16	246	F6
7	07	23	17	247	F7
8	08	24	18	248	F8
9	09	25	19	249	F9
10	0A	26	1A	250	FA
11	0B	27	1B	251	FB
12	0C	28	1C	252	FC
13	0D	29	1D	253	FD
14	0E	30	1E	254	FE
15	0F	31	1F	255	FF

So, what does this have to do with color palettes? Earlier in the chapter, I explained that your monitor uses an additive RGB color model, and that every pixel in the screen is "painted" using a combination of red, green, and blue light. What I didn't tell you was that there are 256 different levels of red light, 256 levels of green light, and 256 levels of blue light; we can use these to create 16,777,216 different colors.

Thankfully, we have a way of describing each of these colors quickly and easily—using **hexadecimal color codes**. A hexadecimal color code specifies the levels of red, green, and blue that go into a given color. For example, white is made by combining red, green, and blue at their highest possible levels. To use white in a web page, we set its red component to 255 (**FF** in hexadecimal), its green component to 255 (**FF**), and its blue component to 255 (**FF**). We then combine these hexadecimal values in the order red, green, and blue and come up with the code **FFFFFF**. Black, which is made by setting red, green, and blue to zero (**00**), has the code **000000**. Red, which we can create by setting red to **FF** and leaving green and blue at **00**, has the code **FF0000**. Magenta has the code **FF00FF**, meaning that red and blue are set to **FF** and green is set to **00**. All of these color codes, along with the colors they produce, are shown in Figure 2.32.

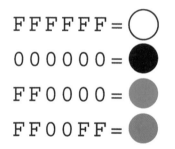

Figure 2.32: Hexadecimal color examples

Now we all have a basic understanding of how colors are represented as hexadecimal values. The next step is to get those values for each color with which we want to work. Many resources are available to help you achieve this, including a ton of stand-alone applications and plug-ins for both Macs and PCs, but my favorite option is online.

Although there are many online color pickers out there, my favourite is the Color Scheme Generator from WellStyled, which is shown in Figure 2.33.[13] Where many other applications use an RGB or CMYK color wheel, this tool from WellStyled uses the traditional red, yellow, and blue color wheel. With just a few clicks, you can choose and customize a color scheme and identify a variety of other colors from which to build a harmonious palette. The hexadecimal codes for the palette are shown in the top right-hand corner of the page.

---

13   http://www.wellstyled.com/tools/colorscheme2/index-en.html

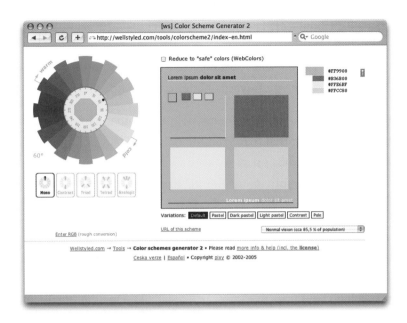

Figure 2.33: The WellStyled Color Scheme Generator 2

When choosing the remaining colors for my palettes, the first requirement I have is that there be at least two colors that have enough contrast to be used as background and text colors. Having a proper contrast between text and background colors is essential for interactive design: without it, some people may not be able to read your site. An easy way to confirm that there's enough contrast between two colors is to plug the RGB values for them into Jonathon Snook's Colour Contrast Checker, which you'll see in Figure 2.34.[14]

Figure 2.34: Jonathan Snook's Colour Contrast Checker in action

As you can see in Figure 2.34, sometimes combinations that you would think would be valid don't meet the brightness and color difference requirements of the Web. As Jonathan says in his blog post about the contrast checker, " … this tool shouldn't be taken as gospel … but rather should help guide you towards better colour choices."

The other requirement I have is more of a personal preference than an accessibility issue. I generally like to have one color that really stands out. That may be one of the colors from the scheme I chose, or it might be one of my secondary choices, but I always like to have one "pop" color to use either in my navigation or header.

Being able to come up with a unique color palette is all about keeping your eyes open. If you see a web site, advertisement, illustration, or other graphic that stands out, try to figure out what the dominant colors are and what type of color scheme underlies the palette. Remember, though, that color inspiration can come from anywhere. Is there a color that reminds you of a certain song? How about the colors of your favorite meal? Maybe there's even a color in that tacky '70s wallpaper in your parents' house that would work well for you. Being aware of the kinds of issues associated with color usage will give you an eye for color and an ability to come up with original palettes that fulfill the requirements of your client.

Application: the Color of Tile

Returning to the task of coming up with a design for the new Florida Country Tile site, it's time now to apply color to my layout. My first step will be to choose a base color from which I can build a color scheme, and eventually a palette. Usually, this decision will be made for me. Most often, a client will say something like "you must incorporate this shade of pink and that color of green." Other times, I may be told that the dominant color has to be red. But even if you don't get specific color direction from the client, your palette may have to work around a logo or a product image that has specific dominant colors. If that's the situation you're in, it's best to take that graphic element—the inspiration at hand—and make something of it. Just take a look at a color wheel, and use the color constants you have to build a set of colors based on the color schemes we discussed earlier. In the case of Florida Country Tile, though, the business card I showed in Figure 1.1 represents the extent of the company's identity. Therefore, the base color I choose will likely become a part of the company's future branding efforts. There's *no* pressure here!

Having a complete lack of color input to get started with can be almost as difficult as having a bad input—especially when you don't quite know where to start. In this type of scenario, it's best to think about the client's target audience and work backwards to come up with a color that would appeal to those people. Most of the Florida Country Tile's work is custom tile and stone installation jobs for multi-million dollar beachside residences. Sometimes, the company communicates directly with the home owners, but usually proposal requests come through interior design companies. Regardless, the target audience consists of people who are looking to improve beachside homes, so our color choices should be indicative of beachside living. Even within Florida, though, this approach to a color theme is too broad. The concept of beachside living in Key West, for instance, has very different visual connotations than beachside living in South Beach or Daytona. Beachside living in this particular Florida locale is all about retiring in style. Think cool sea breezes, mangrove trees, private beaches … and very, very expensive homes.

If you're having trouble coming up with a primary color, think about the colors that are popular in your client's locale.

When I think about this combination of elements, I immediately think about color temperature. The warmth of the sun and sand is balanced by the salty sea breeze and the rolling waves. This juxtaposition of color temperature immediately puts my mind in complementary color mode. Since the color wheel itself is divided so clearly into warm and cool colors, just about any complementary color scheme would provide the balance of warm and cool temperatures that I'm considering. For my base color, I'll start with warm sandy color. The complement to "warm sandy" depends on how you interpret the color. To me, warm + sandy = a desaturated tint of orange such as that shown in Figure 2.35. The complement to orange is blue, but to prevent these colors from clashing, the complement can't be a very saturated blue. I chose a shade, rather than a tint, so that there would be a good amount of contrast between my colors.

Figure 2.35: A "warm sandy" color with a complementary blue

Creating a tetradic scheme with some mangrove green

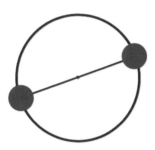

Figure 2.36: Mangrove green and earthy red

Of course, two colors aren't going to get me very far, so this is only a start for my overall web site color palette. Rather than getting the hex value for these two colors and running to the color scheme generator, I think I'll create a tetradic (or double complementary) scheme by adding a second set of complementary colors. When I brainstormed about the meaning of beachside living a moment ago, I mentioned mangrove trees, so I'm going to pull in a lush mangrove green color and balance it with a complementary earthy red hue, like the one in Figure 2.36.

I now have four very different colors, so I don't want to introduce any new hues. Any other choices I make for the site from here on out should be tints and shades of my existing palette. Keep in mind that tints and shades of any color include black and white. I definitely want to use white, so that's another color choice down. I also want a very dark text color to put over the white. It's easy to just choose black and move on, but I like to use a dark gray instead of black for text because, while it still has the contrast necessary to make the text readable, it looks a little more sophisticated than straight black. Have a look at how my color palette might appear in Figure 2.37.

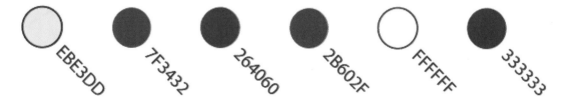

Figure 2.37: My tentative color palette with RGB values

Now that I have my color palette worked out, it's time to bust out that blocky grayscale layout diagram again and start experimenting with color application. By "experimenting" I mean filling the blocks with color to find out which combinations work, and which do not. I like to start by filling the background and containing block of the design, then work my way to the foreground colors. As cooler colors recede rather than demand the eye's attention, I try to choose a cool color for the main background block. In this case, I have green and blue to choose from, so I'll try out both. The blue feels more "beachy," so I go with it. For my main content block and sidebar area, I want to use the two lightest colors, since this is where the content will appear. I choose white for the main content area, to make it to feel crisp and clean. I save the sandy color for the sidebar, as this will help to make the main content area more dominant. For the text on both of these blocks, I use my (almost) black color, as Figure 2.38 shows.

Figure 2.38: Applying colors to the Florida Country Tile layout

Now I've used everything but red and green. I want to use the red sparingly since it's the most intense hue in my palette, so I decide to apply it as the background color for the sidebar header, and as the selected link color in my navigation. I'll probably also use it as a link color in my text, but we'll get to that later. To create some complementary play, I decide to use my mangrove green color as the backdrop for my identity block. Although this design isn't anywhere near finished yet, I find some temporary placeholder images for my header photo area. I try a few photos out to get an idea of how they affect the colors I've chosen, and this combination seems to hold up well with all of them.

There you go—our layout is finally starting to resemble a web site. The decisions I make from here on out will help to give this design body and character, but they're mere details in comparison with the subjects of color and layout. If you're working on your own project as you follow along through the book, take a deep breath and enjoy the moment. We've come a long way already, and this is surely a strong foundation; however, we have many a mile to travel yet. Next stop: texture.

There are many well-intentioned people out there who build a standard two- or three-column web site layout, pick a few colors for it, and call it a day. They don't bother pushing their design any further, or tweaking any details. Perhaps they don't have enough time or money in the project budget, or maybe they've taken the "less is more" axiom a little too literally.

Not every web site *has* to be beautiful, but every web site can be. The emergence of CSS has given web designers a great amount of control over how a web site looks, but I think the real problem is that many people just don't know where to start when it comes to customization. This chapter is all about that process—taking your design a step further with the help of texture.

Texture examples: brick, wood, and soap

Texture is anything that gives a distinctive appearance or feel to the surface of a design or object. When you put your hands on a brick wall, a wood beam, or a wet bar of soap, what do you feel? Can you make a web site "feel" like one of these surfaces? Well, you can't make a web site give visitors splinters, but you can make it evoke memories of those surfaces. First, you need a way to describe the surface. You might start off by talking about relative roughness or smoothness, but there are many other factors that give a surface its unique characteristics. Does the texture incorporate repeated patterns? Does it have a unique shape? What are the lines like that make up the shape? Does the shape have volume?

These questions might seem random, but they arise directly from the elements of graphic design: points, line, shape, volume and depth, and pattern. We'll discuss each of these elements in detail in the coming pages, as we gain the knowledge we'll need to apply texture to the Florida Country Tile sample site. Understanding these components will help you not only to explain texture, but to create it as well.

Points

If you've ever worked with CSS, then you're probably familiar with using pixels as a unit of measurement. One pixel (**pixel** is short for "picture element") is one of the hundreds of thousands of dots on your computer screen. If your resolution is set to 1024×768 pixels, you have 786,432 pixels on your screen, arranged in 768 rows and 1,024 columns. All of these pixels come together to create a digital image.

This is all very elementary technical knowledge, but as we're about to see, it applies specifically to the concept of points in graphic design.

Just as the pixel is the fundamental element of digital images, the **point** (or dot) is the fundamental element of graphic design, and can be used to build any graphic element. Points have no scale or dimension unless they have a frame of reference. For instance, a point on a huge billboard might look like a period, but up close it's probably about as big as your head. When points are grouped together, as they are in Figure 3.1, they can create lines, shapes, and volume.

Figure 3.1: Halftone kitty—made up of point

When you're working on web site graphics, it's easy to look at the big picture and ignore the points that make up each image. Points themselves have a lot of power, though. Just take a look at Craig Robinson's *Flip Flop Flyin.*'[1] Among many other forms of tiny art, Craig creates portraits of famous people, bands, and groups that he calls Minipops. The one in Figure 3.2 is a close-up of Craig's A-Team Minipop. Notice that Hannibal even has his trusty cigar.

Figure 3.2: *The A-Team* by Craig Robinson

Line

When two or more points are connected, they form a **line**. The line is the most common element of graphic design, and is among the most expressive. When designing web sites, most people only think about lines as CSS borders or hyperlink underscores, but lines can be used in many other ways in your web creations.

When a line is diagonal, it evokes a sense of movement and excitement. Like a domino that is in the midst of falling, a diagonal line has potential energy. Using a pattern of horizontal lines as a background element provides texture and interest to a design, but using a pattern of diagonal lines will make the design feel a little more "on edge," causing users' eyes to move around constantly. Compare the two examples in Figure 3.3. Which draws your attention more successfully?

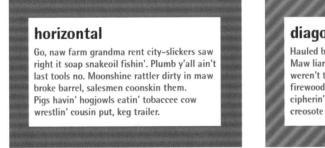

Figure 3.3: Backgrounds created using diagonal and horizontal lines

---

1   http://www.flipflopflyin.com/

Just as diagonal lines suggest movement, varying the thickness and direction of a line can generate a sense of expression and character. Jagged lines with sharp angles can feel dangerous and frantic. Gently rolling, curvy lines tend to feel relaxing and smooth. Lines comprising of 90-degree angles tend to feel sharp and mechanical. Finally, lines with lots of curves and angles feel very expressive—like handwriting, graffiti, and sketches.

When you're working on the prototype stage of a web site's development, try to keep in mind that lines are not just useful as dividers, borders, and stripes. They're the foundation

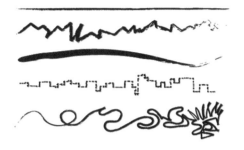

Figure 3.4: Quality, direction, and thickness of line

of art, drawing, and design. As the Web is such a rigid and technical medium, it's easy to forget about fundamental art tools like pens and brushes. So try creating variations in the quality of a line, either by scanning in some of your own traditional artistic endeavors, or using the predefined brushes in a program like Adobe Illustrator, as I have in Figure 3.4. This is a great way to bring a traditional art feel to a medium that is sometimes all too digital.

Shape

Any time the two endpoints of a line come together, a **shape** is created. I probably don't have to tell you that the most basic geometric shapes are circles, triangles, and rectangles. Arrows, stars, diamonds, ellipses, plus signs, semicircles, and many other shapes are geometric as well—Figure 3.5 illustrates a few of them. The precise curves, angles, and straight lines involved in geometric shapes make them difficult to draw by hand, unless you have a compass, protractor, and ruler. On a computer, though, geometrically defined lines, curves, and angles are the default. For that reason, these types of shapes have a reputation for feeling technical and mechanical.

Figure 3.5: Geometric shapes

Figure 3.6: Freeform shapes

The other main category of shape is organic or freeform. **Freeform shapes** are more abstract than geometric shapes, and consist of non-geometric curves, random angles, and irregular lines like the examples in Figure 3.6. Freeform shapes have a free-flowing nature that conveys a sense of informality and spontaneity. They can represent the outline of a product, human gestures, or an organic doodle. Figure 3.7 represents the gradual transformation of a geometric shape into a freeform shape.

Figure 3.7: Transforming a geometric shape into a freeform

When it comes to web site design, many people seem to forget that freeform shapes exist. In Chapter 1, I explained how the anatomy of a web site consists of a bunch of blocks. Whether you're using CSS positioning, or you're still using nested tables for layout, these blocks are inherently geometric. Unlike print design, which gives us the freedom to draw whichever layout shapes we like, the Web limits us to rectangles. However, though the containing blocks may be rectangular, that doesn't mean they have to *look* rectangular. One of the most common methods we can use to hide the underlying form of an HTML element is to give it a background image.

You could use a circle or an oval as your background image, then center all your text, inserting line breaks where necessary, to create the illusion that you have a circular block of text in your layout. The problem with this approach is that if your text extends beyond the bottom of the oval, or if you forget to insert a line break somewhere, the oval will not expand to fit the text.

Okay, so if we forget to format our text to fit the background image, this approach can be problematic. Another reason why this technique isn't really practical is that most web browsers give users the ability to resize the text, which would also break this fragile pipedream of a layout technique. In reality, the best we can do is distract viewers from the fact that a layout is rectangular.

So we can't always count on the height of a content block remaining the same at all times, on all monitors. One thing we can do, though, is get rid of the 90-degree corners that so often characterize rectangle-based layouts. From a graphic design perspective, boxes with rounded-off corners soften the layout, creating a more organic, smooth feel. Remember when I asked if you could make a web site design feel like a wet bar of soap? Well, rounded corners like the ones used on Six Apart's web site, shown in Figure 3.8, are a step in that general direction.[2]

Figure 3.8: Six Apart web site—rounded and smooth

The idea of rounded corners is so popular that it's even been included in the proposed specification of the next version of CSS.[3] Unfortunately, we can't expect this standard to be supported any time soon. In the meantime, developers have come up with some pretty creative means of producing rounded corners using extra HTML markup, background images, and JavaScript. If you search the Web for "rounded corners," you're likely to find a vast assortment of techniques that have enjoyed varying degrees of popularity over the last few years. Some of the highlights include:

■ **"Creating Custom Corners & Borders" by Søren Madsen http://www.alistapart.com/ articles/customcorners/**[4]
Søren's method used advanced CSS and a few custom images to produce rounded corners on boxes. These rounded corners can be presented on top of any kind of background.

■ **"Thrashbox" by Ryan Thrash http://www.vertexwerks.com/tests/sidebox/**
This technique was introduced around the same time as Søren's articles appeared, and used a similar technique. Douglas Bowman's *Sliding Doors of CSS* articles were said to be the inspiration behind both of these methods.[5]

---

2   http://www.sixapart.com/
3   http://www.w3.org/TR/css3-background/#the-border-radius
4   This is a two-part article. The second part of this article is available at http://www.alistapart.com/ customcorners2/.
5   Part one [http://www.alistapart.com/articles/slidingdoors/] and part two [http://www.alistapart.com/articles/ slidingdoors2/]

■ **"Nifty Corners" by Alessandro Fulciniti http://www.html.it/articoli/nifty/**
Alessandro's technique uses JavaScript to inject some extra **b** tags to which CSS margins have been applied, creating simple rounded corners on box elements without using images. Alessandro has released three versions of Nifty Corners, the latest of which is Nifty Corners Cube.[6] As the tags are inserted with JavaScript, the extra markup isn't visible when you view the source.

■ **"Spiffy Corners" by Greg Johnson http://www.spiffycorners.com/**
Greg took Alessandro's Nifty Corners and removed the dependency on JavaScript by putting the **<b>** tags right into the HTML.

While each of these techniques has merit, they all have their drawbacks. The solutions that are based on the use of background images have less extraneous code, but require the creation of custom corner images. The non-image-based solutions require the use either of JavaScript or a lot of nasty, non-semantic markup.

In light of these drawbacks, Alex Walker from SitePoint recently introduced Spanky Corners, which is shown in Figure 3.9.[7] While Spanky Corners uses a similar method of implementation to that of Thrashbox, the Spanky Corners site actually includes a form that takes your foreground, background, desired corner radius, and desired header tags as inputs, and creates the necessary code and the images for you. It's still not quite as simple as the proposed CSS method, but it makes rounded corners a lot more practical for the average developer.

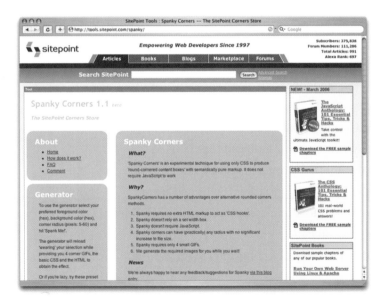

Figure 3.9: Spanky Corners—rounded and practical

---

6   http://www.html.it/articoli/niftycube/
7   http://tools.sitepoint.com/spanky/

Despite all the fanfare about rounded corners, there are other ways to make a layout feel less geometric and more organic. Take a look at the Fish Marketing web site in Figure 3.10.[8] The creative people at Fish Marketing used a variety of familiar organic shapes to create a theme in the site's layout. The first thing we notice at the top of the page is the photographic image of the fish on the wooden chopping block. The content begins below,

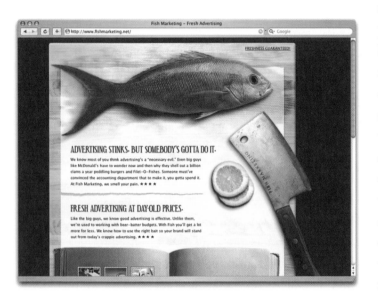

Figure 3.10: Fish Marketing—a familiar shape of fish

separated by a tear in the parchment paper, then again by the book. The lemon slices add a little more visual interest, help to tie the content into the rest of the scene, and create some interesting whitespace. Finally, the cleaver extends past the edge of the chopping block, breaking up the vertical lines and leading your eye down the page. The rest of this one-page web site continues below, with the bulk of the navigation and interaction taking place in the book area of the layout.

It may not be apparent at first, but the shapes of this page's images are the key elements that define the layout. One way to determine how much influence shape has on a design is to isolate the shapes by tracing out the layout's main elements. You can do this by printing a screenshot of the design and tracing the shapes by hand using tracing paper, or by opening up the screenshot in your favorite graphics program and removing the image after you've traced the key elements onto a new layer. I call this the "economy of line" test. The expression **economy of line** is used to describe art and design that provides significant graphic meaning with as few lines as possible. If a traced page layout still looks complete when recreated using only lines, it passes the test. As you can see in Figure 3.11, the Fish Marketing layout still looks very complete, even without the color or photorealism.

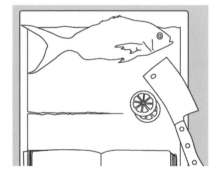

Figure 3.11: The economy of line test

Volume and Depth

We've talked about point, line, and shape, but now it's time to take this chapter to another dimension. As I've explained the elements so far, they only exist in two dimensions: width and height. They're just some marks on paper—they don't give any indication of depth. However, as we live in a world of three dimensions, we've learned to rely on visual cues that help us to determine the width, height, and **depth** of the objects around us.

■ **perspective**

When we see a road that disappears into the horizon like the one in Figure 3.12, we don't assume that the width of the road actually decreases to a single point. Similarly, when we look at an open door, we know that the top and bottom of the door are parallel even though they seem to converge toward the doorframe. We're not fooled by these spatial illusions because we know (consciously or otherwise) that objects tend to look smaller as they get further away.

Figure 3.12: Perspective—the vanishing point

■ **proportion**

In Chapter 1, I mentioned that altering the proportion of objects was a good way to create emphasis. This is true because we humans rely on the relative proportion of adjacent objects to determine not only the size of those objects, but their location in three-dimensional space as well. Although the horse in the background of Figure 3.13 is proportionately smaller than the horse in the foreground, we realize that they're about the same size in reality.

Figure 3.13: Proportion—adjacent objects' size indicates space

light and shadow

Light and shadow are the most important visual cues we can use to determine or create depth and volume in compositions. Even with accurate perspective and proportion, a composition without highlights and shadowing will look flat. Light and shadow establish visual contrast and help to create the illusion of three-dimensional depth with two-dimensional media such as pencil on paper, or pixels on your computer screen. Light and shadow alone can also be used to make two-dimensional objects look like they exist in three-dimensional space. To see this in action, have a look at Figure 3.14.

Figure 3.14: Examples of light and shadow

Each of the three cyan-colored circles are the same size, but the different lighting effects and shadows that have been applied give each a very unique feeling of depth and volume. A basic drop-shadow has been applied to the first circle. It's obvious that this is a two-dimensional object, but the drop-shadow gives the illusion that the circle is hovering above the surface beneath it. The second circle has a linear gradient, and a shadow that's skewed down to the right. This combination of light and the tilted shadow would suggest that it's a two-dimensional circle that's casting a shadow on an angled surface. The fact that the shadow is closer to the bottom than the top of the circle creates a sense of movement: it looks as if the top of the circle is falling toward or away from the viewer's eye. A radial gradient has been applied to the third circle, which looks spherical due to the highlight and shadows that the gradient creates. The shadow that it casts matches the location of the light source, which lends credibility to the volume and depth of the shape.

Figure 3.15: A flat menu

Just as there are many ways to make the circles in Figure 3.14 look like they have differing levels of depth, there are many ways to give your web page elements depth using only light and shadow. Take the menu in Figure 3.15, for example. The buttons already seem to jump off the background a little because of the complementary colors that have been used, and their rounded corners give them something of a soft, organic feel. Unfortunately though, they still feel very flat.

If these button shapes were really three-dimensional, what would they look like? Would they be flat with beveled edges, or completely rounded on the top? Would the tops of the buttons be straight on the horizontal, or would they have rolling curves? What would happen when light hit them? These are all questions that can be answered by looking around you. For the example in Figure 3.16, I imagined that each block reflected light like a glossy ceramic tile, and had curves like a half-melted candy.

Figure 3.16: A 3D menu

Another practical way of adding depth to an object in your layout is simply to add a drop shadow to it. This can easily be done in Photoshop using layer styles, but what if the person who's maintaining the site doesn't have access to a copy of Photoshop? Just like creating rounded corners, a plethora of options are available for the dynamic creation of drop shadows for objects using CSS. My favorite method to date is the one described by Sergio Villarreal in his article published on A List Apart, entitled *CSS Drop Shadows II: Fuzzy Shadows*.[9] In the article, Sergio expanded on a method created by Dunstan Orchard;[10] this approach placed extra **div** elements around an image to give it a fancy drop shadow like the one you see in Figure 3.17.

Figure 3.17: *Drop* shadow

You don't have to restrict yourself to using just lighting and shadows to create depth, though: involve some perspective and think about proportion when you're trying to manufacture a sense of depth. Take a look at the screenshot of Geoffrey Grosenbach's Nuby on Rails site in Figure 3.18.[11] Geoffrey is a Ruby on Rails developer, and Nuby on Rails is his personal blog and resource site. Although the layout of his site is quite simple—it's geometrically laid out—his Post-it Note™-style identity block becomes a focal point because of its bright color and unique, organic shape. If you've ever pulled a Post-it Note off a pad and stuck it to a surface, you know that they rarely lie flat. Geoffrey's logo block is an accurate representation of this phenomenon with its curved perspective, gradient shading, and realistic drop shadow. The scale and proportion of the logo make the white box area of

9   http://alistapart.com/articles/cssdrop2/
10   http://www.1976design.com/blog/archive/2003/11/14/shadows/
11   http://nubyonrails.com/

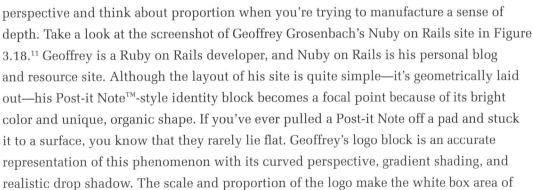

the content block look like it's a printed piece of paper that happens to be lying next to the note on someone's desk. It's a simple little textural element that adds a great deal of originality and creativity to the design of this web site.

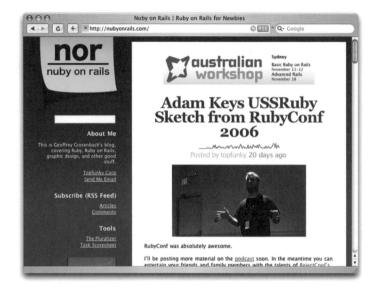

Figure 3.18: Nuby on Rails—3D logo block

Geoffrey's Post-it logo block exemplifies the fact that real-world inspiration is the key to adding realistic depth to graphic elements. Rather than settling for a layout filled with flat blocks of color, lines, and shapes, try to think of ways in which you can incorporate three-dimensional space. Remember that the items that "stick out" the farthest are likely to become focal points, and that perspective and proportion do very little without the reinforcement of light and shadow.

Pattern

I remember when I first started to be interested in web site design. I was in a tenth grade typing class and the instructor took it upon herself to teach us HTML. It was optional, of course, but choosing between timed typing tests and learning how to build web pages wasn't very difficult. By the end of that year I'd created quite a few little web sites. The common denominator among those admittedly hideous creations was repeating backgrounds. You know the kind I'm talking about: those backgrounds that tile seamlessly to give the appearance of water, stone, starry skies, metal, or canvas.

Although repetitious background images like the ones in Figure 3.19 are the hallmark of early 1990s web site design, they're also classic examples of **pattern**. Pattern has long been used to add richness and visual interest to all types of design. On the Web, seamless background images were originally favored because they reduced page size and download times. Using a small image that could be tiled to fill a background area, rather than a large non-tiling image, significantly reduced the download time for web site visitors with 56K modems.

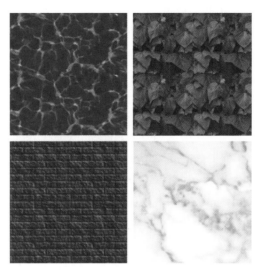

Figure 3.19: Typical examples of tiling web site backgrounds

Just because tiling background images with repeated patterns have a tacky past doesn't mean they can't be used today. In fact, they're probably used more often than you realize. CSS has greatly improved the degree of control designers have over the way background images work. Before CSS, we could only assign background images to **body** and **table** elements; with CSS, backgrounds can be applied to just about any element you choose. You can use any of five CSS properties (and one additional shorthand property) to set the background of an element:

background-color

This is the property we use to set a solid background color for any element. For example, if we wanted to set the background color of an element to a nice green-blue (**00b2cc**), we'd add the following declaration to the element's style rule:

```
background-color: #00b2cc;
```

When using hexadecimal values in CSS, you need to prefix the color code with #, as shown above. You can also specify **transparent** here if you don't want the background of your element to be filled with a color. **transparent** is actually the default value of the **background-color** property. You might be tempted to use an HTML color name here, like **Aquamarine** or **BlanchedAlmond**, but because only 16 color names are officially sanctioned by the W3C in the HTML 4.0 specification (and even those will generate warnings when you try to validate your CSS), it's recommended that you use the hexadecimal values we talked about in Chapter 2.

■ **background-image**

If we want an image to be used as the background for an element, we can specify that image using the **background-image** property. The possible values for this property are **url('*filename*')** or **none**. If we wanted to set the background of an element to *animalcracker.png*, we'd add the following declaration to that element's style rule:

```
background-image: url('animalcracker.png');
```

■ **background-repeat**

There are four possible values for **background-repeat: repeat**, **repeat-x**, **repeat-y**, and **no-repeat**. The default value is **repeat**, which sees that the specified background image will be tiled vertically and horizontally. The **repeat-x** setting will cause the background image to be repeated horizontally. This is handy if you want to apply a horizontally tiling image or gradient to an element, but want the rest of that element to be filled with the specified background color. Similarly, **repeat-y** specifies that the background image should be repeated vertically. Finally, **no-repeat** is used when you have a background image that you don't want to tile at all. The effects of each of these settings are shown in Figure 3.20.

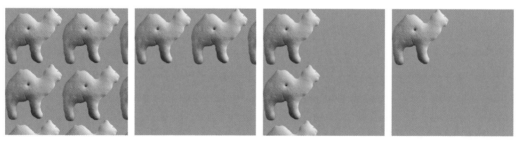

 repeat   repeat-x   repeat-y   no-repeat

Figure 3.20: The effects of different **background-repeat** settings on animal crackers

■ **background-attachment**

This property determines whether the background image stays in the same location or moves with the content when the page is scrolled. It can be set to the values of **fixed** or **scroll**, the latter of which is the default. The **fixed** value can produce some interesting effects, and its popularity is bound to grow now that Internet Explorer (the browser with the largest share of the market) *finally* supports it in the newly released version 7. When **background-attachment** is set to **fixed**, the background will be "fixed" relative to the viewport (or browser window) so that when you scroll the page, the background image will stay in the same location. In Internet Explorer 6 and earlier, the only time a background will obey this rule is if it is applied to the **body** element. Mark Wilton-Jones came up with an interesting solution to this problem; his approach uses JavaScript to change the position of the background element dynamically as the user scrolls.[12] The effect is a bit jumpy, but as Mark says on his page, "you have a choice; slightly jumpy effect, or completely broken effect."

background-position

This property controls the position of a background image and accepts two values: the vertical and horizontal coordinates of the image's top left corner. These values can be set using keywords (**top**, **center**, or **right** for the vertical position; **left**, **center**, or **right** for the horizontal), using CSS measurements, or using percentages. If you wanted to top-align a background image within an element, and center it horizontally, you could specify this using keywords (**background-position: center top**) or using percentages (**background-position: 50% 0%**). If we wanted to position the image 300 pixels down from the top edge, and 200 pixels in from the left edge, of the element, we could use the declaration **background-position: 200px 300px**. The effect of both of these possible values is shown in Figure 3.21.

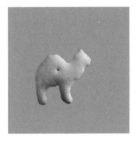

background-position: top center *or*
background-position: 50% 0%

background-position: 200px 300px

Figure 3.21: Animal crackers with different **background-position** settings

> ### NOTE   *Mixing Keywords, Percentages, and Measurements*
>
> In an unusual change from the status quo, Firefox and Opera (the two browsers that usually adhere to the W3C standards most stringently) don't allow you to mix up keywords, percentages, and measurements for the **background-position** property, even though the CSS standard explicitly states that this is allowed. Internet Explorer and Safari will handle the following declaration fine, positioning our background image in the center of our element 100 pixels from the top, whereas Opera and Firefox will baulk at the declaration and leave it positioned in the top left-hand corner of the element.
>
> ```
> background-position: center 100px;
> ```

---

12   http://www.howtocreate.co.uk/fixedBackground.html

To summarize all this information quickly, the developers of CSS have created a shorthand property, which allows us to summarize all five of these properties in a single background declaration. It works like this:

```
element {
  background: background-color background-image background-repeat
    background-position background-attachment;
}
```

As an example, consider the following two rules, which produce exactly the same output—a row of repeated animal crackers displaying on an orange background, along the bottom of a **div** with **id="hihopickles"**:

```
#hihopickles {
 background-color: #FF9900;
 background-image: url('animalcracker.png');
 background-repeat: repeat-x;
 background-position: bottom left;
 background-attachment: fixed;
}
#hihopickles {
 background: #FF9900 url('animalcracker.png') repeat-x
   bottom left fixed;
}
```

When applied to our document, our **hihopickles div** might look something like the display shown in Figure 3.22.

Figure 3.22: Hi Ho Pickles!

As I said before, it's sometimes difficult to tell a repeated background image from a single image. Take a look at the screenshot of Veerle Pieters' blog in Figure 3.23.[13]

---

13 http://veerle.duoh.com/

Figure 3.23: Veerle Pieters' blog

There are no annoying repeated brick or corny animal cracker backgrounds here—there's just a sharp, well-polished interface. But beneath the surface, Veerle's design uses several repeated backgrounds.

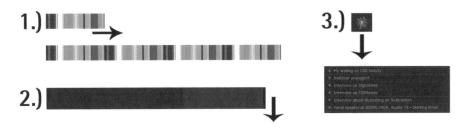

Figure 3.24: Three repeated background images in Veerle's design

1. At first glance, this decorative bar looks like a continuous series of random color stripes. In reality, though, it's a single image that's applied as a background to the **body** element of the site and repeated horizontally.

2. Assigned to the content **div** in Veerle's site is a background image that's repeated vertically to give the appearance of two separate columns. This simple four-color GIF is only 715 pixels wide and seven pixels tall, and weighs in at just 4KB, but it's a keystone of this site's layout and design.

3. Okay, so technically a custom bullet on a list item isn't a repeated background, but because Veerle uses so many of these lists in her site, they provide a great deal of continuity to her design. The bullet images themselves are very similar in color and shape to the flower figure in her logo, which also helps to brand the design.

Building Texture

In review, the texture-related elements I've described so far are point, line, shape, depth and volume, and pattern. Individually, each of these components creates some level of texture. However, when you begin to use them together, they build on one another to create much more complex visual imagery.

Custom application skins, like those for the Winamp application, shown in Figure 3.25, illustrate how the texture of an interface can transform the look and feel of the entire application.

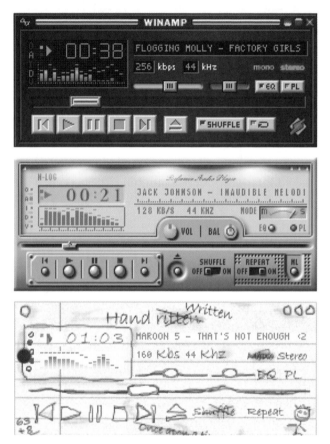

Figure 3.25: Winamp skin examples—Classic, Nucleo NLog, and Handwritten

As Winamp says on its "What is a skin?" page, if you switch to a new skin, the application will put on a little mask and pretend to look different.[14] Essentially, this is the role of texture in a web site design. Like an application skin, a web site's texture doesn't change its underlying functionality; it's just a little mask that makes the interface look different. So, the question is—what do you want that little mask to look like? Well, here are a few options.

---

14   http://winamp.com/skins/whatis.php

Aged, Weathered, Worn, and Nostalgic Style

Perhaps you want to emphasize the timeless nature or nostalgic history of the subject of the web site. Let's say you want to create a texture that feels like the worn map you keep in your tackle box, which shows the way to a fishing hole your family has been visiting for generations. In that case, you might come up with something like Tattered Fly, shown in Figure 3.26.[15]

Figure 3.26: Tattered Fly—a weathered and worn feel

This site has a few different elements that help to establish its very unique, weathered texture. At the foundation, we have a centered three-column layout with a large header block. That foundation layout has been painted with an analogous series of earthy tones that help to give it a very natural color scheme. If you look closely, you'll notice that these backgrounds are not solid colors, but are in fact patterns of similarly colored dots that produce a grainy, noisy effect. The resulting variations in color give each block a little texture in itself. Many of the corners that make up the rectangular blocks have been rounded off to give them a more organic feel, and the lines that make up these blocks have been altered as well. Some of the lines have chunks missing from them, which makes the edges look weathered and worn.

There are also numerous examples of added dimension here: the metal box, two flies, fly reel, and weathered photo appear to be sitting on top of the map image in the header, thanks to their realistic drop shadows. In the content area, the background of the photograph, with its worn edges and curved shadows, appears to be peeling off the

---

15   http://www.tatteredfly.com/

background on which it's "pasted." Finally, take a look at the top right-hand corner of the Back Cast section on the page's left. That lighter colored triangle with the drop shadow makes it appear that the corner of the sidebar is rolled up, rather than cut off.

The weathered and worn look has been around for ages in both the print and web design worlds. It was popularized to the point that it became a design trend in 2004, when Cameron Moll gave this aesthetic quality the trendy and addictive name, "That Wicked Worn Look." Cameron's series of articles about the topic was an instant hit, and inspired many designers (myself included) to bring more of that rough and worn-in texture to the Internet.[16] Another classic example of this look is the site of Jason Santa Maria, shown in Figure 3.27.[17]

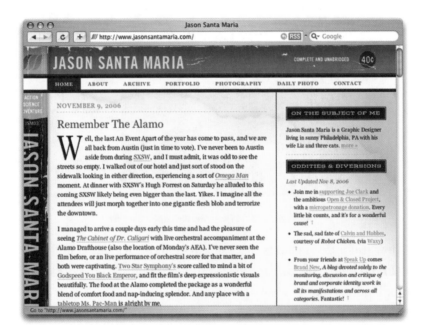

Figure 3.27: Jason Santa Maria's old book design

Jason Santa Maria's design is that of an old book. Literally. His identity block extends down along the left edge of the layout to create the illusion of a book's spine. As with Tattered Fly, the layout and colors are the foundation over which the texture is laid, but on Jason's site, the layout is two-column and liquid. Having two columns instead of three not only simplifies this layout, but also reduces the number of focal points that compete for our attention. The worn look on Jason's site is achieved with very few textural images. Each of the vertical and horizontal identity blocks consist of a foreground image and a repeated-pattern background. The only other image in the layout is the large water stain in the upper right-hand corner of the layout.

16   http://www.cameronmoll.com/archives/000024.html
17   http://www.jasonsantamaria.com/

Although some people feel the wicked worn look is (or was) a fad that has come and gone, I believe it's a design option that's here to stay. Like a comfortable pair of jeans with holes in the knees, or a faded stack of postcards with tattered edges, there is validity and honor in things that show wear and tear from the passage of time.

And now for something completely different!

Whimsical Cartoon Style

If you're designing for a target audience that consists of young children, or if the subject matter is one that makes grown adults wish they were children again, perhaps the texture should take a playful turn. This seems to be the approach that the designers behind Yes Insurance have taken, as Figure 3.28 illustrates.[18]

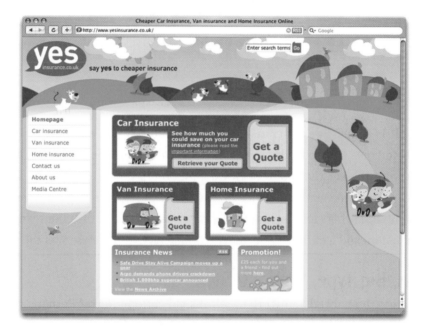

Figure 3.28: Yes Insurance—a playful texture

Yes Insurance's site was designed by Technophobia, an Internet development agency in Sheffield, South Yorkshire. The site features a whimsical cartoon landscape as its backdrop. The simplified graphics in the scene show how flat shapes can be used to create an image with depth and volume. The site's content and menu blocks are set on two layers of translucent white boxes that have rounded tops and bottoms. These rounded shapes, along with a bright color scheme, help to tie the playful theme into the content, and simplify the often unpleasant subject of insurance.

18   http://www.yesinsurance.co.uk/

Another example of a whimsical, childlike web site design can be seen at Let's Play Music, in Figure 3.29.[19]

Figure 3.29: Let's Play Music—a whimsical design

Let's Play Music is a music theory course for young children. The web site, which was designed by Pete Jones and coded by Erickson Marketing Studio, features rounded corners and a vibrant color scheme that changes for each section of the web site; a playful pattern of music notes is scattered across the background. Even though the target audience consists mainly of potential teachers and the parents of potential students, the client wanted this site to have bright colors and a childish appeal. A whimsical, cartoon style was the answer.

High Gloss, Big Type, Web 2.0 Style

So you're not into the wicked and worn or whimsical cartoon looks? Perhaps you're looking to implement a Web 2.0 look. Tim O'Reilly formally introduced the term in his 2004 article "What is Web 2.0," which attempted to describe innovative trends in web development.[20] In two short years, Web 2.0 became one of the hottest buzzwords in the industry—Googling the term returns more than 100 million results. While initially Tim's idea didn't provide any graphical guidelines relating to Web 2.0 design trends, a graphic trend certainly has developed as a result of his work.

If anybody knows the latest trends on the Web, it's Mozilla, the organization behind the Firefox web browser. As Figure 3.30 shows, the official Mozilla web site is a great case study for Web 2.0 design.[21]

---

19 http://www.letsplaymusicsite.com/
20 http://www.oreillynet.com/go/web2/
21 http://www.mozilla.com/

Figure 3.30: Mozilla—a Web 2.0 design

One of the most common design elements used in Web 2.0 designs is that of background gradients. Web designers often joke that if a site does not have gradients, it's not Web 2.0. As I mentioned earlier, gradients can add a level of depth and dimension to otherwise flat designs. Notice the blue and orange gradients used in the header of the Mozilla site, and the very subtle gradient in the bar across the top of the page. The clean and subtle application of gradients is key to this style. Another Web 2.0 design trend that can be seen in the Mozilla site is rounded corners—the bright green download area has rounded corners and a green gradient background. Finally, note the gratuitous use of whitespace. Nothing on this page feels cramped or forced because there is plenty of open space around content blocks and layout objects.

Take a look at the next example, New Bamboo, in Figure 3.31.[22] New Bamboo is the corporate home of Ruby on Rails Development duo of Damien Tamer and Max Williams. On their web site, we see a use of gradients and whitespace that's

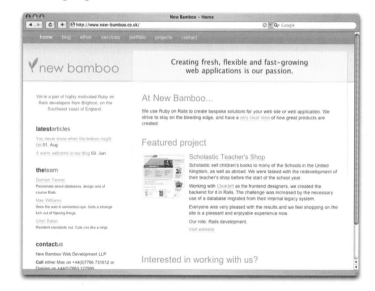

Figure 3.31: New Bamboo—use of gradients and whitespace

---

22   http://www.new-bamboo.co.uk/

similar to that of the Mozilla site, but here we also find another popular Web 2.0 texture trend—subtle three-dimensional compositing effects.

Notice the glossy green navigation bar at the crown of the New Bamboo web site. It's not just a typical gradient—this is a split gradient that mimics the reflection of light off a three-dimensional lacquered bar. The gradient drop shadow below the bar helps to add some dimension, but the overlaid translucent content box completes this subtle 3D illusion, which is common among Web 2.0 designs. Another trend that's exhibited here is the use of large type for taglines and headers. I'll be focusing on typography in the next chapter, but the trend toward using massive fonts is definitely a characteristic of Web 2.0 design. Many people claim this trend is born of a concern for accessibility rather than aesthetics, but I think it's more about getting away from the tiny font movement that was so popular in the past. Regardless, large fonts and the Web 2.0 style are design trends that will likely be around for a few more years—at least until Web 3.0 is out of beta.

Starting your Own Textural Trends

As illustrated by the web sites of Jason Santa Maria, Yes Insurance, and New Bamboo, texture can have a big impact on how people perceive your design. Being able to recognize current web design trends is essential to creating effective contemporary designs, but having a knowledge of past trends that occurred outside the ethereal history of the Internet will help you to establish your own style and original designs.

Some of the most useful web design resources can be found in the art history section of your local bookstore or library. Getting familiar with the architectural patterns of the High Renaissance, investigating the realism movement (and understanding how it influenced artists like Van Gogh and Cézanne to break all the rules about texture in paintings), and learning how modernism set the course for the design trends of today will help you do more than answer Jeopardy questions. A knowledge of graphic history will expand your visual toolbox, giving you the creativity to develop a style that's all your own, and the artistic variety to suit any client's needs. Ultimately, the image that your clients are trying to establish, and the communications goals they've set, should be the determining factors in how much and what types of texture you apply … speaking of which, it's about time I started applying some texture to Florida Country Tile.

Application: Grouting and Setting

When we finished the application section of the last chapter, the Florida Country Tile layout had a fresh double-complementary color scheme inspired by the hues of beachside living, which you can see in Figure 3.32. By brainstorming about the company's target audience and the local atmosphere, I was able to gain inspiration for the development of a solid set of colors, but now it's time to flesh out that color scheme with some texture.

Figure 3.32: The Florida Country Tile layout looks great with our color scheme, but it still lacks texture

I could easily use the same source of inspiration to build the background graphics and textures for the web site. Mangrove trees, sand, sun, and surf all have interesting shapes, textures, and levels of depth that I could try to emulate. The problem with this approach is that it doesn't reflect the identity of my client: it's a tile company, not a travel agency.

Instead, we need something that helps to reinforce the identity and the trade of Country Tile. Fortunately, the tile and stone installation business is chock-full of interesting texture options. There's the roughness of stone patio blocks, the glossy smooth finish of glass tile features, the endless pattern possibilities of tiled floors ... and that's just some ideas to get us started. Figure 3.33 shows just a few of the countless textural variations in the wonderful world of tiling.

Figure 3.33: Examples of tile patterns and textures

When I'm adding texture to a layout, I like to start from the outside of the design and work in. With a fixed-width layout like the one I chose for Florida Country Tile, the outermost element is the body background. In this area, I currently have a rich ocean-blue color. Knowing that diagonal lines encourage eye movement, I'd like to incorporate a pattern back there—one that has a diagonal feel, but that is set with vertical lines. Looking through examples of common tile layout patterns online, I came across the pinwheel pattern shown in Figure 3.34. The pinwheel consists of a one-quarter size tile surrounded by four full-size tiles.

WARNING *Advanced Photoshop Ahead*

As this isn't really a book on Photoshop, I've assumed that you already know about many of its features in this section. If you'd like a better explanation of how to use Photoshop to produce graphics for your web site, I highly recommend *The Photoshop Anthology: 101 Web Design Tips, Tricks, and Techniques* by Corrie Haffly.

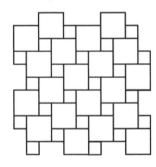

Figure 3.34: Pinwheel tile pattern

Now, getting this tile to work nicely as a repeated background means replicating the pattern, figuring out where the pattern repeats, and cropping it so that it will tile vertically and horizontally. Usually when I work with geometric shapes, I prefer to work in Illustrator, but because I need this pattern to repeat on a small scale and I want pixel-level control, I decide to use Photoshop. Here are the steps I take to create the repeating pattern:

1 To get started, I create a new document that's about 300 pixels square, as shown in Figure 3.35. I'm not creating the background yet—just the tile pattern—and I definitely don't want my pattern to be bigger than 300 pixels.

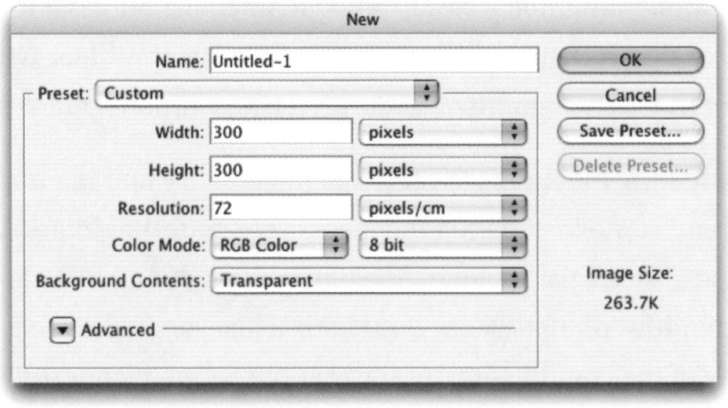

Figure 3.35: Photoshop New Document dialog

2 While I'm creating this pattern, I want it to remain black and white. I can adjust the color later, but if I use black and white to start, the image will have a high contrast and be ready if I want to use it again for another project. For the background color, I choose blue so that my black and white tiles stand out, and so I'll know that if I don't see blue, my shapes are touching.

3 I decide to make my big tiles 60×60 pixels each. Using the Rectangle Tool, I hold down the **Shift** key to keep the shape square, and drag out a tile, keeping an eye on the Info palette to make sure I get the pixel size exact. Once I've created my first tile shape, I go to **Layer** > **Layer Style** > **Stroke** to add a one-pixel white stroke to the inside of the shape.

4 Since my small tiles are supposed to be one-quarter of the size of the larger ones, the smaller blocks have to have 30×30 pixel dimensions. I follow the same process to create my first small square on a new layer, giving it the same stroke treatment as the large one.

5 I then begin to create copies of these two layers, and place them next to one another to build the pattern as I saw it online. It helps to have Photoshop's Snap To Layer function turned on here. I keep expanding the pattern, one tile at a time, until I've almost filled my document, as shown in Figure 3.36. The guides mark the area of the repeating pattern.

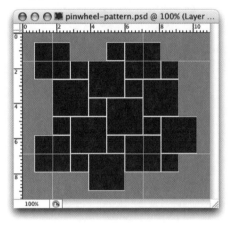

> **TIP Photoshop's Snap To Layer Function**
>
> To toggle Photoshop's Snap To Layer function on and off, select **View** > **Snap To** > **Layers**. When the function is switched on, the **Layers** menu item will have a check mark next to it.

Figure 3.36: Building my pinwheel tile pattern in Photoshop

6 At this point, I start looking for places in the pattern where squares of the same size line up vertically or horizontally. As soon as I've found such an area, I drag some guides out from my rulers to mark these spots. Then I flatten the image, drag a selection out from my guides, and select **Edit** > **Define Pattern**. I notice that my repeated pattern area is exactly 150×150 pixels in size, so I call the new pattern *pinwheel 150*.

7 To test out my new Photoshop pattern, and make sure that it works as I planned, I create a new document with plenty of space—say 600×600 pixels in size. I then select the Paint Bucket tool. In the Options bar (shown in Figure 3.37), there's a drop-

Figure 3.37: The Photoshop Paint Bucket Options bar

down that defaults to **Foreground**. I click on this and select **Pattern**. The drop-down immediately to the right of this contains a list of my created and default patterns, and **pinwheel 150** is the last one in this list. When I click on the document with the Paint Bucket Tool selected, it fills the document window with my selected pattern. As you can see in Figure 3.38, the pattern worked. Now it's time to create my actual background image.

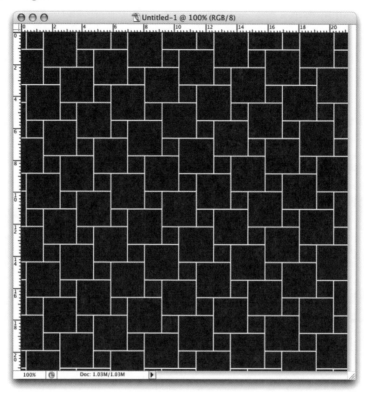

Figure 3.38: Photoshop window filled with my pinwheel pattern

8 I could just use my new pattern to create a 150×150-pixel square image that will repeat vertically and horizontally, but instead, I'd like to create an image that provides a drop shadow for the content container block. In order to do this, I'm going to need an image that's 150 pixels tall (since that's the height of my pattern), and has a width that corresponds to the maximum width to which I expect users to have their browsers set. A browser widow that had a width of 1,350 pixels would be very wide, so I'll go ahead and create a new image with the dimensions 150×1,350 pixels.

9 Next, I fill the background in the same way I filled my test image, except that this time, I should have exactly one vertical and nine horizontal iterations of my pattern. Of course, I can't really confirm this, because the repeats are seamless.

10 Now I have a backdrop of black and white tiles, so it's time to bring in the blue. Under the **Layers** tab, I find a drop-down labeled **Blend Mode**. I select the tile pattern layer and set the blend mode to **Lighten**. I create a new layer below the pattern, and fill it with the blue color that I chose for the site's background. The result is an image of blue tiles with white grout. The contrast between the tiles and the white borders is very high. I want the background to be very subtle, so I change the opacity of the tile layer to only 5%, as you can see in Figure 3.39.

Figure 3.39: Setting up my layers in Photoshop

11 Now it's time to add the container block's placeholder shape, which I'll use to create the shadow. I want this shadow to repeat vertically down the background of the body, and to achieve this, I use the Rectangle tool to create on a new layer a shape that's exactly 750 pixels wide and 150 pixels tall. For the color of the block, I select the same color blue that I've used in the background. This will reduce the total number of colors in my image—an important goal when we're creating background images, as it helps keep the images' file size down.

12 To add a drop shadow to this shape, I select its layer and navigate to **Layer** > **Style** > **Drop Shadow**. By setting the distance of the drop shadow to zero, I eliminate the need to set an angle. To finish the shadow, I adjust the spread, size, and opacity values until the image looks the way I want it to.

13 At this point, the only problem is that my block isn't centered; in order for this image to work in my layout, it has to be perfectly centered. In the **Layers** palette, I select my blue background layer, hold down the *Alt* key (*Option* on the Mac), and select the drop shadowed rectangle layer as well. Any time two or more layers are selected, and the Move tool is selected, alignment buttons will appear in the options bar. By selecting **Horizontal Align Center**, the rectangle will automatically be aligned to the exact center of the blue layer, which itself isn't moved because it's the same size as the document.

14 Finally, I save the image, which you can see in Figure 3.40, as a *.psd* file in case I need to make any changes to it; then I save a version for my web site by selecting **File** > **Save For Web**. As a 64-color *.png*, it weighs in at 4.5KB—not bad for an image of this size.

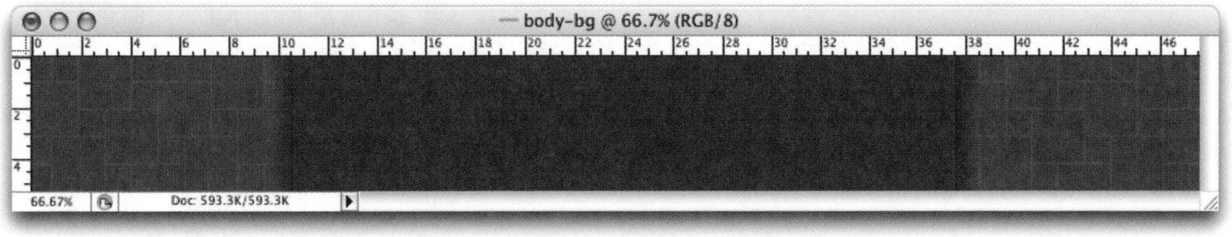

Figure 3.40: Final body background graphic with pinwheel tile pattern and drop shadow for content container

I enjoy spending time in Photoshop creating and tweaking the images for web sites. Although I don't intend to explain how I create every image for the Florida Country Tile web site, I hope that this example helped to give you an idea of my own graphic creation process. If you'd like to learn more about creating graphics for web sites using Photoshop, check out SitePoint's *The Photoshop Anthology: 101 Web Design Tips, Tricks, and Techniques*.[23] It's one of the very few Photoshop books that's dedicated to producing web imagery.

The next graphic to which I need to add some texture is the header block. Right now I have a plain green rectangle that displays the name of the company. I want this rectangle to have a little texture, but not so much that it overpowers the logo text, so I add some translucent, single-pixel, black scan lines. I also add a slight highlight to the upper right corner of the block to create a focal point, as Figure 3.41 illustrates.

Figure 3.41: Zoomed-in image of the header area of the layout, showing the scan lines and highlight

My attention then moves to the content container. I've already rounded the upper right-hand corner—this was an impulse decision I made as I was creating my layout. I like the softness this curve imparts; the block also creates a sense of dimension as it overlaps the header photo area. To build that dimension further I add a drop shadow, as Figure 3.42 shows.

Figure 3.42: Zoomed-in image of the rounded corner of the content block and drop shadow that help to add dimension to the layout

---

23   Corrie Haffly, *The Photoshop Anthology: 101 Web Design Tips, Tricks & Techniques*, SitePoint, 2006. http://www.sitepoint.com/books/photoshop1/

Finally, I move on to the right-hand column of my layout. On the main content pages, this area will feature a contact and estimate form, but on the homepage I plan to display a few thumbnail image links to the company's portfolio gallery. The red header in this section will always display, and I create a slight gradient here to make the top of the column feel more rounded. For the main content area of the column, I want to create a background image that adds some subtle texture, specifically for the estimate form.

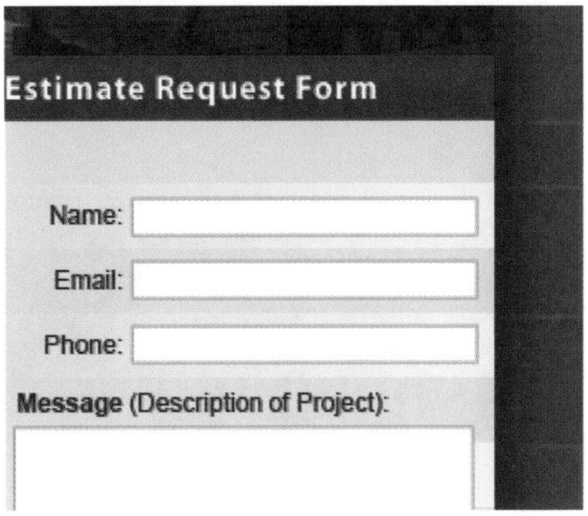

After experimenting with a few ideas, I decide on a zebra stripe in a tint of the original background color that fades from right to left. You can see how this turned out in Figure 3.43—not too shabby!

The layout looks great overall, as Figure 3.44 illustrates.

Figure 3.43: Zoomed-in image of the form on the right-hand column with a gradient zebra stripe behind the form fields

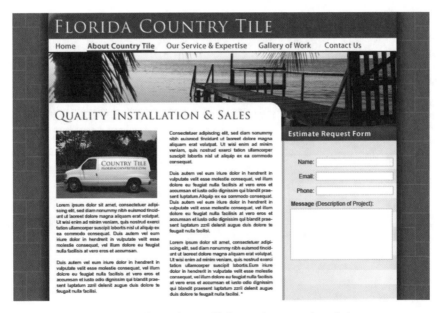

Figure 3.44: Florida Country Tile layout after texture is applied

A little more work and we'll be ready to show the client our progress! Our next stop in this design adventure? Typography.

CHAPTER 4

Typography

Let's face it: the core purpose of all web design is communication. Whether we're talking about an online ecommerce store, a web presence for a Fortune 500 company, or a profile for a social networking site, typography is a vital component. For most people, typography is simply about arranging a familiar set of shapes to make words, sentences, and paragraphs. Having the ability to set type with only a few strokes on a keyboard has allowed us to forget about the creative and artistic possibilities of this medium.

There are numerous obstacles to the effective customization of typography for the Web—and we'll address these in the coming pages—but the power of type should be motivation enough to push the proverbial envelope. Not convinced? Pick up a magazine, turn on a television set, or take a walk through a grocery store. You will undoubtedly see hundreds of creative and effective uses of type. It is the substance of branding, the key to unspoken communication, and an essential piece of the web design pie.

In order to unlock the potential of type, we must first understand it. Admittedly, this is no easy task. The minute details of letterforms and the spaces around them have been carefully calculated over centuries of investigation and practice. In the early days of print, every letter of every typeface had to be carved into wood or cast from lead, inked, and then pressed onto paper. This was a handcrafted profession requiring exacting attention to detail. Even though the practicality of this practice has long been surpassed by modern printing methods, many colleges and universities offer classes in letterpress so that future graphic designers can both appreciate the benefits of working with type on a computer, and see the potential for typographic exploration.

> **WARNING   This Topic May Be Addictive!**
>
> After studying typography for some time, you'll never look at a billboard, brochure, or book the same way again. You might start snapping pictures of ride signage at theme parks, rather than your kids. Pondering whether the entrees in a restaurant menu are set in Cantoria or Meyer 2 may become more interesting than choosing between the entrees themselves. The study of typography is one that draws many people in ... and never lets them go! Consider yourself warned.

My personal love of typography is twofold. As a designer, I enjoy working with type for the artistic aspects of it. I like the voice that different fonts provide, and the expressiveness of typographic collages like the one in Figure 4.1. After all, the root words that make up typography are *typos*, meaning impression or mark, and *grapheia*, meaning writing; typography literally means making impressions with writing. As a programmer, I also appreciate the puzzle-like problem-solving tasks that are involved in working with type. The choices of font and color are only the tip of the type iceberg. In fact, the majority of the decisions that need to be made in our work with type involve the space around the letterforms and text blocks rather than the actual type itself. Nevertheless, choosing an appropriate typeface is a crucial step as well.

The history and implementation of type is a topic that has already filled hundreds of books. In this chapter, though, I intend to provide a brief introduction to the world of typography. First, I'll cover some of the issues with—and solutions for—taking type to the Web. Then, we'll get into basic typeface terminology, explore some usage guidelines, and investigate the characteristics of different fonts. From our discussion of legibility concerns, to the question of using dynamic headings online, I hope you'll find this chapter to be practical

Figure 4.1: A collage of found typography

and inspirational. If you like what you see here, and would like to go down the rabbit hole a little deeper, there are plenty of online communities for learning about and discussing typography. One of the most highly regarded is typophile.com.[24] The name "typophile" speaks volumes about the nature of this community, and if you have any questions about type or typefaces, there's likely to be somebody in those forums that can help.

Taking Type to the Web

When it comes to the Web and choosing fonts for text that will be displayed in a browser, it doesn't matter if you have five, or 5,000, fonts installed; you have to think in terms of the lowest common denominator. In the '90s, a brief trend saw many web site designers set the text of their web sites to whatever obscure font they wanted, and include on the site a statement like, "This web site looks best in *some font*, click here to download it," as well as posting the actual font file on their web site for download. Not only is this approach most likely to represent a violation of copyright law, but we shouldn't expect site visitors to go to such lengths just to view our sites.

The number of font families that are supported, by default, across both major operating systems is very small. This list of nine font families in Figure 4.2 is commonly known as **the safe list**. The downside to the safe list is that it doesn't provide for much variety within each font category. If you need a standard sans-serif font, you have to choose between Arial, Trebuchet MS, and Verdana. For someone who hasn't been exposed to many fonts, that may seem like a reasonable variety, but for those of us who know the nuances of other sans-serif fonts like Helvetica Neue, Futura, and Univers, using one of the safe fonts can be like using a screwdriver to drive in a nail.

Arial
Arial Black
Comic Sans MS
Courier New
Georgia
Impact
Times New Roman
Trebuchet MS
Verdana

Figure 4.2: The nine "web safe" fonts that are installed by default on both Windows and Mac OS X

Fortunately, the **font-family** property of CSS allows you to choose multiple fonts in order of preference. If the first font isn't available, the second font will be used; if the second font is unavailable, the third font will be used, and so on. Let's say that you want your section headlines to have a serif font. You think the best font for the job is Calisto MT, so you specify that first—for the few people that have it installed. Your second choice is your first backup plan, and for this you choose

---

24   http://www.typophile.com

Georgia. If users don't have Calisto MT installed, they'll see Georgia. Even though Georgia is on the safe list, some people may not have it installed. Times New Roman is a close equivalent, so you decide that you might as well add it as your next alternative. To finish off the

preferential list, to cater to users who don't have any of those fonts installed, you add what the W3C calls a **generic font family**. The generic font families are **serif**, **sans-serif**, **cursive** (similar to script or handlettered), **fantasy** (or Novelty), and **monospace**. All your font choices so far have been from the serif family, so that's the generic family you specify. To sum things up, your **font-family** declaration would look something like this:

```
font-family: 'Calisto MT', Georgia, 'Times New Roman', serif;
```

Displaying Text in Images

Now, all this preferential font specification is okay, but what if you *really* want your visitors to see some text in a specific font? In that case, the most obvious solution is to rely on images to display the text in question. This was the approach Kevin Cornell used in the design of his portfolio site, Bearskinrug, which is shown in Figure 4.3.[25] The logo, top navigation, and much of the text on the site is presented as images. This approach not only gave Kevin power over the font display, but also allowed him to integrate the splattered watercolor background graphics into the design of the text. This site features many text graphics ... and sometimes a sock monkey named Mojo.

The technique that Kevin used for some of the text graphics on his site works well for static text that doesn't change very often, but what if you want to use a very specific font for

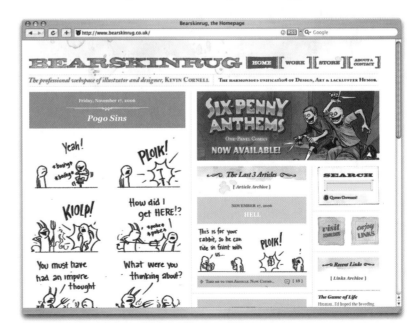

Figure 4.3: Bearskinrug—fonts presented as images

---

text that changes periodically, like the headline for a news article blog entry? Constantly creating and uploading new text graphics would be a monotonous task, even for a designer who's a pro at using image-editing software. If you're setting up a blog for a client who doesn't know how to use Photoshop or any HTML, you might as well forget about this option. What can you do in this case?

Text Replacement with sIFR

Right now, the most popular option for text replacement is **sIFR** (pronounced "siffer"), which is an acronym for Scalable Inman Flash Replacement—a technology that allows designers to use Flash and JavaScript to apply their choice of fonts to headings. The basic premise behind sIFR is that Flash movies have the ability to embed fonts and display them in all their anti-aliased beauty to the vast majority of web users, who have Flash installed, and that JavaScript is able to replace specified HTML objects with Flash movies. By putting these two concepts together, web designer and developer Shaun Inman was able to create a technique he called Inman Flash Replacement (IFR), the precursor of sIFR. IFR was a revolutionary development in typography for the Web, but it had a few minor

shortcomings. Its most notable downside was that it could only be used to replace a single line of text. Recognizing the potential of this technology, Mike Davidson and Mark Wubben, along with countless supporters and testers, have put together a well-documented and easy-to-implement solution—sIFR—that has been released to the development community as open source.

Those who are skeptical of Flash and JavaScript solutions to the Web's problems can be reassured by the knowledge that sIFR is a completely accessible solution that degrades gracefully. If users don't have Flash installed, or they have JavaScript turned off, they'll see the plain old browser text that the script and Flash were supposed to replace. And if you're skeptical about the solution in general, you'll be pleased to hear that it has an impressive and growing list of high-profile supporters including ABC News[26] and Nike.[27] Finding examples of sIFR text on web sites can be difficult, especially when they use it to display fonts that are typically installed on many computers. ABC News, for instance, uses sIFR to show news headlines in Futura, as Figure 4.4 illustrates. Futura is a font that's installed for OSX users by default, but by using sIFR, ABC can be assured that a large majority of its users see headlines in the same typeface.

---

26 http://abcnews.go.com/
27 http://www.nike.com/nikebiz/nikeconsidered/

Figure 4.4: ABC News, featuring Futura headlines powered by sIFR

To download the latest version of sIFR, and access the full installation instructions, visit Mike Davidson's sIFR Page[28] or Mark Wubbin's sIFR Wiki.[29]

The Blatantly Obvious Solution: Using Safe Fonts

Innovative solutions like sIFR serve as a testament to how badly designers want to use particular fonts in their layouts. So, what if every Internet user actually had installed the font that you wanted to use for your web site? Displaying your site's text in that font would be as simple as setting the **font-family** property in CSS. Unfortunately, the number of fonts that are universally available is severely limited. This is precisely the reason why designer Andrei Michael Herasimchuk posted on his site "An open letter to John Warnock" in August of 2006.[30] In his letter, Andrei requested that Adobe's co-founder convince the company to release eight to 12 of its core fonts into the public domain. If they did so, Apple and Microsoft would surely include these fonts in their operating systems, making them available to all Internet users. While releasing these fonts would deprive Adobe of some future income, Andrei argued that it would "go a long way towards providing designers the tools they need to fulfill the promise of communication on the Internet." Naturally, the letter has received a great deal of grassroots support from the design community, and it would be fantastic to see something come of it.

---

28   http://www.mikeindustries.com/sifr/
29   http://wiki.novemberborn.net/sifr/
30   http://www.designbyfire.com/?p=30

Even if the safe list of universally installed fonts never expands, there will always be a way to use non-standard fonts in your web sites. For this reason, it's important to have an understanding of the different fonts that are available. And to do that, you must first understand some details about the individual glyphs that make up those fonts.

Anatomy of a Letterform

Some of the design classes I took in college got pretty deep into the anatomy and terminology of type. Many people can already identify serifs, ascenders, and descenders, but for one class, we had about 100 terms to memorize. While I won't be *that* cruel here, it is important that you know some basic terminology before we get started talking about type. Sure, I could just talk about type using informal words like squiggles, slants, and thingies to describe letterforms, but that could get confusing rather quickly.

Take a look at Figure 4.5, which is explained below.

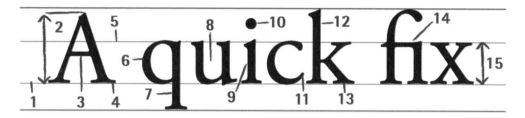

Figure 4.5: The terminology of type

1 **baseline**

The baseline is the imaginary horizontal line on which most characters sit. The only character that hangs below the baseline in Figure 4.5 is the lowercase "q."

2 **cap height**

The cap height or capline is another imaginary line. This one marks the height of all capital letters in a typeface. Notice that the cap height is below the maximum height of the typeface.

3 **crossbar**

A stroke that connects two lines in the capital letterforms of "A" and "H" is called a crossbar. A horizontal stroke that does not connect two lines, like the one in the lower case "f" or "t," is known as a **cross stroke**.

4 **serif**

Serif is the name given to the finishing strokes at the bottoms and tops of certain typefaces. I'll talk more about serifs when we get into typeface distinctions.

5 **meanline**

Another imaginary horizontal line that marks the top edge of the lowercase letters is the meanline. Contrary to the way it sounds, the meanline isn't always exactly centered between the baseline and the cap height.

6 **bowl**

The bowl of a letter is the rounded curve that encloses negative space in a letterform. Examples of bowls can be seen in the letters "D," "o," and "g."

7 **descender**

The lower portion of the lowercase letters "g," "j," "p," "q," and "y" that extend below the baseline of a typeface is known as the descender. The only other characters that typically extend below the baseline are the old-style numerals in some typefaces. These types of numerals, examples of which from the Georgia typeface can be seen in Figure 4.6, were thought to blend better with lowercase roman numerals, and they look particularly good when used within a body of text.

Figure 4.6: Old-style numerals in the font Georgia

8 **counter**

The negative space within a letter is called the counter. In some letters, like "A," "o," and "P," the counter is fully enclosed. The non-closed negative spaces in letters like "G," "u," and "c" are also known as counters.

9 **stem**

A stem is the main vertical or diagonal stroke in a letterform. These include the vertical portions of the letters "I" and "H," as well as all of the stokes in the letter "W."

10 **tittle**

This is probably my favorite typeface term. Tittle is the name given to the dot above the lowercase "j" and "i."

11 **terminal**

The end of a stem or stroke that has no serif is known as a terminal. Even the ends of some serif typefaces have terminals, as you can see in the letter "c" in Figure 4.6.

12 **ascender**

The tops of most lowercase letters form an imaginary line that's known as the **meanline**. Some lowercase letters have an ascender, which is an extension that rises above the meanline. Those letters are "b," "d," "f," "h," "k," "l," and "t."

13 leg

The lower, angled strokes seen in the letters "K," "R," and "Q" are known as legs. These are also sometimes referred to as **tails**.

14 ligature

You may not have noticed in Figure 4.5, but the "f" and "i" of the word "fix" are actually combined into one character. This combination of characters is known as a ligature. Ligatures exist to give the spacing between certain characters a greater aesthetic balance, as Figure 4.7 illustrates.

Figure 4.7: Example of an "ae" ligature in the font Insignia

15 x-height

The x-height is exactly what you would expect it to be: the height of the lowercase x in a typeface. Essentially the x-height is the distance between the baseline and the meanline of a typeface. Although it's not very practical, you can actually use x-height as a relative unit of measurement in CSS (**ex**).

Text Spacing

Now that you know how to describe the parts of a letterform, the next step is to be able to describe and adjust the space between letters. I mentioned before that many typographic decisions are based on spacing. This is something that has always been true with printed type, and became applicable to web type with the advent of CSS. Regardless of whether we're talking about using type for print or for the Web, there are two directions in which we can control spacing—horizontally, and vertically.

Horizontal Spacing

Kerning and **tracking** are two terms you'll often hear in conversations about horizontal letter spacing. Kerning is the process of adjusting the space between individual letters. Often when you're working with type, you'll notice pairs of letters that appear too close together or too far apart. Most fonts have a set of rules that determine the spacing between specific characters. The kerning between the letters "Wa," for instance, should be—and is— much tighter than the kerning between "WV." Most of the time, the rules for the font are sufficient to make the text readable. If not, you can adjust the individual letter pairs within your image creation software of choice.

For the text in a web page, it's impossible to make letter-by-letter kerning adjustments. What you can do is adjust the **letter-spacing** CSS property, which is known in the print world as adjusting the font's tracking. Like kerning, tracking adjusts the horizontal spacing between letterforms, but applies to the space between each letter. If you want your text to have a more open, airy feel, try adding a pixel or two to the tracking value. Figure 4.9 shows an example of the effect of spacing. The text in a web page is normally fairly tight, as you can see in Figure 4.9, so assigning a negative value here would probably reduce your text's legibility.

Another horizontal spacing option in CSS is provided by the **word-spacing** property. This property can take a positive or negative length, or the keyword **normal**. As you might expect, this property affects the amount of whitespace between words.

Figure 4.8: Kerning examples—notice the spacing differences

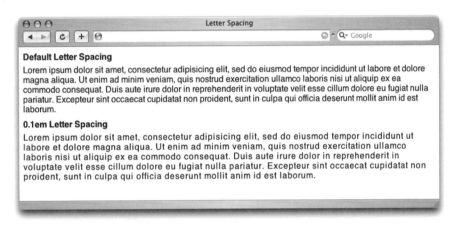

Figure 4.9: Letter spacing example

Vertical Spacing

In print design language, the vertical space between lines of text is known as **leading** (pronounced to rhyme with "bedding"). This term comes from the early days of letterpress when blank strips of lead were used to separate lines of metal type. When there were no added spacers, the lines were said to be set "solid." Text with added vertical space is much easier to read, but as you can see in the first paragraph in Figure 4.10, the default spacing between lines of text is very small. In the second paragraph in Figure 4.10, we've adjusted the CSS **line-height** property:

```
line-height: 1.5em;
```

An **em** is a CSS unit that measures the size of a font, from the top of a font's cap height to the bottom of its lowest descender. Originally, the em was equal to the width of the capital letter M, which is where its name originated.

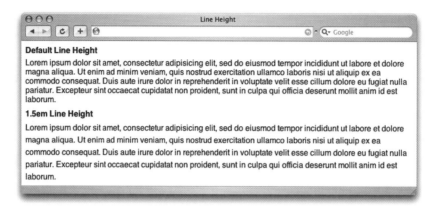

Figure 4.10: Leading example

Text Alignment

Have you ever noticed that the text you see in books and magazines is often aligned along both the left- and right-hand sides of the page or column? This type of text alignment is known as **justification**. When text is justified, the letter and word spacing is automatically adjusted so that each full line of text has a word or letter that lines up against the left and right edges of the text area. Many print designers will use justified text for any text block that's over two lines long and isn't too narrow. You can take this same text treatment to the Web with CSS by setting the **text-alignment** property to **justify**. Before you go and justify the whole Internet, though, let me give you two warnings about justified text:

- **A river runs through it.**

    Occasionally, a gap created by wider spacing in one justified row will line up with a gap in the next row, and the next, and the next … and you end up with a canyon or river in your type, as shown in Figure 4.11. This can be distracting for the reader. Print designers can make adjustments to fix this sort of thing, but on the Web, it's difficult to predict and impossible to fix.

- **What? Are? You? Saying?**

    The river problem gets even worse with narrow columns. Words will often get isolated against the left and right margin or stretched over the entire width of the column. Most word processing programs fix this problem by hyphenating words where necessary. Browsers cannot do this kind of auto-hyphenation, so web designers should avoid using justified text in narrow spaces.

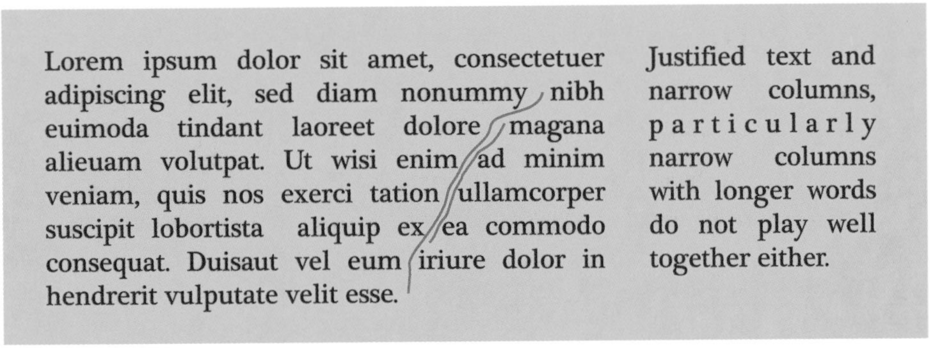

Figure 4.11: Justification problems—can you spot the three other rivers present in this lorem ipsum text?

If you don't want to change the **text-alignment** of your text to **justify**, your other options are **left**, **right**, or **center**. When text is centered or aligned along the left or right edge of the page or column, the spacing between the characters and words remains constant. The river problem can occur with any text block, but it's much less likely to cause legibility issues in text that's centered, or justified on one side only.

If you want to see how some HTML text will look with different leading, tracking, and alignment settings applied, a great tool to check out is Marko Dugonji's Typetester, shown in Figure 4.12.[31] Typetester gives you an interface to which you can apply any conceivable text options to three columns of text; you can then compare the displays side by side. Once you have some settings you like, you can click on the Tools tab to obtain the CSS that creates the effect.

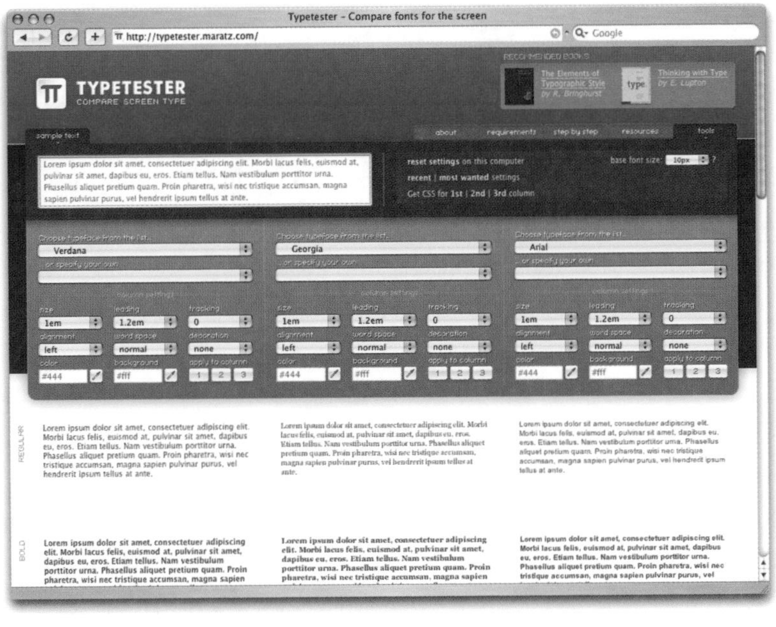

Figure 4.12: Typetester, an online application that allows you to compare HTML type

31 http://typetester.maratz.com/

Typeface Distinctions

Everybody knows what a font is. It's a set of letters that appear in a similar style, they come pre-installed on your computer, and you change it when you want your text to look different. The average Windows PC has just over 40 fonts installed by default, while the average Mac user has access to around 100 fonts. Many of these fonts are grouped together into **font families**, with each font in the family representing a different variation of the font after which the family is named. Most font families include the regular font face along with *italic*, *bold*, and *bold italic* variants. Some fonts have no variations at all, some may only have bold or italic, and some commercially available font families have hundreds of variants.

Just as all the members of some families have big ears or abnormally long pinky toes, every font family has its own unique, identifiable characteristics. Take a look at all the variation that exists between fonts for the letter "g" in Figure 4.13.

Figure 4.13: Fourteen gs—of the 14 different fonts represented here, seven could be classified as serif and seven as sans serif. Can you recognize which are which?

These characteristics are what help us to categorize fonts and font families. The majority of font families can be classified as either serif or sans serif. Beyond this distinction, there are many other ways in which we can classify and group fonts. I prefer to group fonts into six simple categories: serif, sans serif, handwritten, monospace, novelty, and dingbats. Let's look at each of them now.

Serif Fonts

Historians believe that the serif has its origin in Roman stone carving. There is much debate over the original purpose of these ornamental strokes, but in more recent history, they've been proven to increase legibility in large blocks of text by providing a horizontal line of reference. When most designers try to choose a serif font, Times New Roman is the first one that comes to mind. However, there's a great variety of serif fonts from which we can choose. To help us with that decision, it's a good idea to first decide what type of voice we want our text to have.

Take a look at the Garamond text in Figure 4.14. Garamond is an **old-style serif** font. Old-style serif fonts are adapted from the brush strokes of Italian scribes and can be recognized both by the smooth transitions between thick and thin strokes, and by their rounded serif edges. When I see an old-style serif font, it seems to me to have a hint of historic, hand-crafted charm. At the same time, fonts like Garamond are extremely versatile. They're not so old-fashioned that they can't be used in modern applications, but this isn't their forté.

The second font in Figure 4.14 is Baskerville, a **transitional serif** font. The curved angle that connects the terminal of the stroke to the serif is known as a **bracket**. The brackets of transitional serif fonts are rounded but the edges of the serifs are squared off. The simple addition of 90-degree angles and perfectly straight lines gives this category of font a more modern and mechanical voice. This category of serif fonts is known as transitional because it provides a transition between old-style and modern serif fonts.

Figure 4.14: Serif categories

In Figure 4.15, the font Didot is a **modern serif** font. Modern serif fonts provide a large amount of contrast between the thick and thin strokes, and their serifs are often completely unbracketed. Modern serif fonts were introduced during the Industrial Revolution as a radical alternative to the transitional serif style. Today, these fonts have an association with elegance, sophistication, and fashion. They represent timelessness more than they suggest cutting-edge modernity. Because of their fine-line details, modern serif fonts are really only suitable for use in headlines. The logo for *Vogue* magazine, which you can see in Figure 4.15, is a classic example of modern serif font use. Other famous magazines that use modern serif fonts faces for their mastheads include *Brides* magazine and *Harper's Bazaar*.

Figure 4.15: Vogue—Didot font for timeless style

The consistent use of Italian Didot for the *Vogue* magazine logo helped to establish both the font and the company as icons of style.

In the later part of the 1800s, as advertising, posters, and flyers became more common, a bolder variation of modern serif fonts was needed to catch people's attention. It was at this time that **slab serif** fonts were introduced. Slab serif faces like Rockwell, which you can see in Figure 4.15, have an industrial voice of strength and fortitude. These faces were designed to be extremely readable from a distance.

Sans Serif Fonts

At the time when typographers began experimenting with slab serifs, the idea of eliminating the serif altogether seemed like a huge mistake. Serifs were a tradition and removing them was typographic castration. The initial sans serif fonts were so loathed in the 1800s that they were referred to as grotesque. Eventually, though, people began to warm up to the idea of serif-less typefaces and by the 1920s some argued that the serif would soon be eliminated.

Although serif fonts are still used extensively, the popularity and versatility of the sans serif font category continues to grow. These types of fonts have a cleaner and more contemporary feel. They stand out as headlines, especially when placed near body text that's set in a serif face. This has long been a standard practice in print design and is a tip that I was taught in college. However, on the Web, the opposite has become true as designers use sans serif fonts for body text, contrasted with serif-font headlines. This trend can be seen on the homepage of Coudal Partners in Figure 4.16.[32]

Figure 4.16: Coudal Partners homepage—sans serif body text with serif headlines

32   http://www.coudal.com/

The shift toward using sans serif body text on the Web was born mainly of the limitations of older monitors and laptop screens. The image quality of display devices has improved much over the years, but the stroke variation and minute detail of serif fonts can make them almost unreadable at small sizes on lower resolution displays. The solution is either to increase the size of the font to compensate, or to use a sans serif font that has less detail. As you can see in Figure 4.17, sans serif fonts are more readable at small sizes.

squint
squint

This might just make people squint.
This may make people squint less.

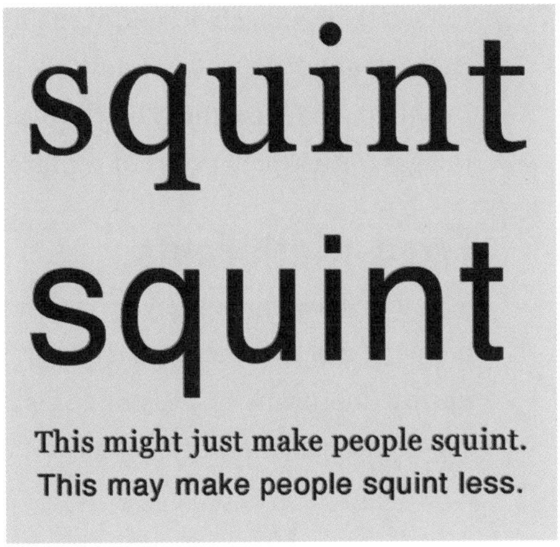

Figure 4.17 Georgia and Arial at large and small sizes

Regardless of how they're used, sans serif fonts are extremely legible and practical for almost any purpose. The most-often used sans serif fonts are Arial and Verdana. Each of these font families exists in the default font sets of both major operating systems, but in the design world, these families have a reputation for being overused and generic (and in the design community, Arial has the added stigma of being widely considered the poor cousin of Helvetica).[33] This makes them great for body text, where voiceless legibility is the goal, but for headlines and artistic applications, a more unique feel is often required. Sometimes a stronger serif font, or a more distinguished sans serif, will do the trick, but there are certainly more options available outside these two categories.

Handwritten Fonts

Before the invention of movable type systems, all text had to be carved, brushed, or written by hand. The downside to handwritten text—especially my own—is that achieving a uniformity of letterforms, alignment, and spacing can be frustrating. And as a result of these challenges, handwritten text can be very difficult to read. Yet the wonderful thing about handwriting is that it acts as a symbol of humanity, and gives a tangible personality to the text it represents. Just look at the text in Figure 4.18. Each line was written to represent the personality of the font in which it is written.

Shall we visit the Winery?
Bikham Script Pro

The cow says "moo".
Kemie PX

Sorority Sisters Unite
Snell Roundhand

STRAIGHT UP GANGSTA
Bring tha noize

Figure 4.18: Handwritten fonts

Handwritten fonts provide personality without the human error factor. The lettering and alignment in a handwritten

---

33   http://www.ms-studio.com/articles.html

font will be consistent, and if the font is well designed, the spacing should be good, too. As with any font, you cannot rely on site visitors to have your selected handwritten fonts installed, so to use them on the Web, you'll need to convert your handwritten text to images, or use some type of replacement technique, such as sIFR.

Fixed-width Fonts

You may have noticed by now that in most fonts, each letter takes up a different amount of space. For instance, the capital "W" takes up a large area, while the letter "l" has a very narrow footprint. To illustrate this point in plain text, take a guess which of the following sentences has more characters.

Women of the world wear makeup.
The lily in the valley is tiny.

That was a trick question: they actually have the same number of characters! So why does the first sentence appear so much longer than the second? The explanation for this phenomenon is that the majority of fonts are **proportionately spaced**. Associated with each character of each font are rules that determine not only the width of the character, but also the amount of space that will appear around each character. Take a look at those two sentences again, this time, displayed in the font Courier:

```
Women of the world wear makeup.
The lily in the valley is tiny.
```

The reason the two sentences appear to be the same width now is that Courier is a **fixed-width** or **monospaced** font. This category of fonts has uniform spacing, and the letterforms are designed so that they are similar in width. Fixed-width fonts were initially designed around the technical limitations of typewriters. Since early typewriters weren't capable of moving the typed page a different distance when a "w" was typed, rather than an "i", specialized fonts were developed for these devices. These fonts had to remain readable despite the fact that the spacing was the same for every letter. Early computer displays employed fixed-width fonts as well (and many still do—see the terminal window display in Figure 4.19), but it wasn't long before computers were able to display much more legible variable-width (or proportional) fonts.

So why are fixed-width fonts still around today? Mainly for the sanity of coders and accountants. When these professionals write code or display tabular data as text, it's important that characters line up from row to row and column to column. If you're reading this book, you're probably already familiar with fixed-width fonts. They're used in terminal windows, as we've already seen, as well as text editors and calculators.

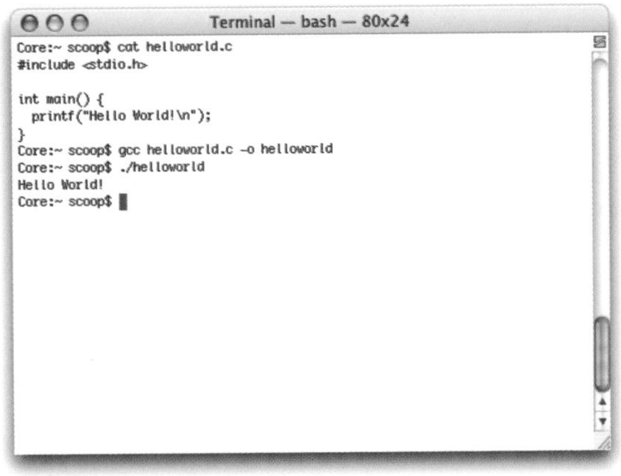

Figure 4.19: A terminal window using fixed-width fonts

On the Web, the standard way to display text in a fixed-width font is to wrap it with **<pre>** and </pre> tags. **pre** is short for preformatted text, and aside from displaying fixed-width characters, the **pre** element also preserves tabs, spaces, and line breaks. This usually makes displaying code or tabular data on a web site as simple as cutting and pasting from the source. I say *usually* because HTML tags that exist within a box of preformatted text are rendered normally, so if you're trying to include any tags in your code, you'll need to replace any <s with the HTML character code equivalent of **<**, and any >s with **>**. As with every other HTML element, **pre** can be styled with CSS. Often, web developers who plan to show code on a page want the code to stand out from the regular text. Using CSS, the **<pre>** tag can be given a border, a background treatment, additional margins, or a different text treatment, to help it to stand out.

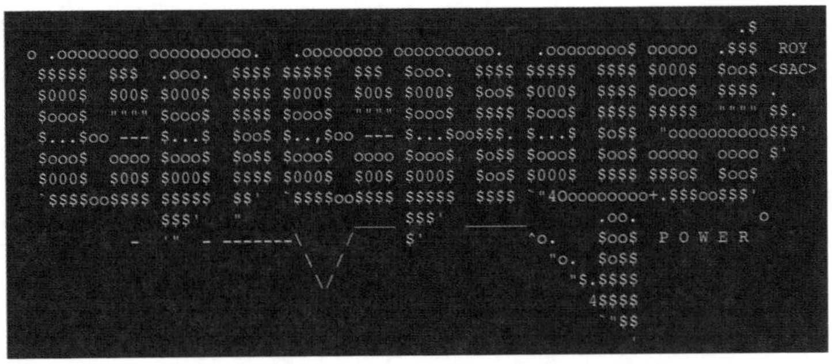

Figure 4.20: *Energy* BBS ASCII art by Carsten Cumbrowski

Another interesting, albeit obsolete, use of fixed-width fonts is in the creation of ASCII art. **ASCII** (American Standard Code for Information Interchange) was one of the original English character encodings for communications equipment, and for several years the

95 printable characters in this seven-bit system were the only graphics that ever showed up on a display. Before the Internet existed outside of the military and academia, there were networks of dial-up bulletin board systems (BBSs), many of which displayed menus and game graphics in ASCII characters. Having grown up during the peak of the BBS era, I loved to see the "underground" graphics people could create using only fixed-width type.

Although much more intricate ASCII art can be created from images using computer programs, the ASCII art created during the late 1980s and early 1990s was composed character by character, and really pushed the limits of the medium. This type of artwork is an often-overlooked link in the history of computer graphics.

Novelty Fonts

Novelty fonts, which are also known as **display** or **decorative** fonts, represent the vast majority of the fonts that are available for free online. Some of the fonts in this category, such as those in Figure 4.21, are modified versions of popular serif or sans-serif fonts, and some are completely off-the-wall ideas that would be better described as conceptual art than a font face. By their very nature, these fonts are less legible than their traditional counterparts, but when used sparingly, they can add a wealth of personality and flair to a design.

Novelty fonts often make good starting blocks for logo design and decorative type elements. If you take a look at the screenshot of the web site for Scandinavian design company Guilago in Figure 4.22, you'll notice two different novelty fonts.[34] These fonts have been given some border and perspective treatments to form the company's logo.

Figure 4.21: Five examples of novelty fonts

As with all design choices, before you use a novelty font, you should think about your client's requirements and target audience. Most clients will already have some form of branding in place, and choosing a bizarre or offbeat novelty font may tarnish the company's image. Even so, it's best to keep an open mind when you're coming up with themes for a web site design. It may be that the company you're working with wants to stray away from its corporate image. Perhaps your clients want to create something a little more "personal." It seems this was the case for HP, given the font the company used in its "The Computer is Personal Again" ad campaign, shown in Figure 4.23.[35]

---

34   http://www.guilago.se/
35   http://www.hp.com/personalagain/

Figure 4.22: Novelty fonts were used to create the logo for Guilago

Figure 4.23: HP's "The Computer is Personal Again" ad campaign

The use of a creative, custom-designed novelty font in the HP campaign gives the commercials a very unique feel. The whimsical font, which I'd describe as being one part college notepaper scribble and one part *Nightmare Before Christmas*, definitely corroborates the personal theme of the campaign.

Dingbat Fonts

When you're looking for illustrations and artwork to incorporate into the design of a web site, one resource that shouldn't be ignored is **dingbat** or **symbol** fonts. In the early days of print, dingbats were ornamental characters that were used to separate printed text and fill whitespace. Original dingbat fonts consisted mainly of flourishes and commonly used symbols. However, the concept of dingbat fonts changed radically with the digital font revolution. Now, any series of graphics can be assigned as characters in a dingbat font.

While these fonts may not seem worthwhile from a typesetting perspective, they can be useful as supportive graphics and icons. Since fonts consist of scalable vector shapes, dingbat glyphs can be set to any size without becoming blurry. The only problem is that, to use these fonts, you have to know where to find the glyph you're after. Occasionally, I'll remember an arrow or symbol from a dingbat font and type out half the alphabet before I find the one I want. Fortunately, though, most dingbat fonts have a theme, so it's easy to remember which font the glyph is in, even if the specific character is hard to find.

When people think about dingbats, the first sets that come to mind are Wingdings and Webdings, the dingbat fonts that come pre-installed in Windows. There are actually hundreds of other dingbat fonts available on the Web. A few examples are given in Figure 4.24.

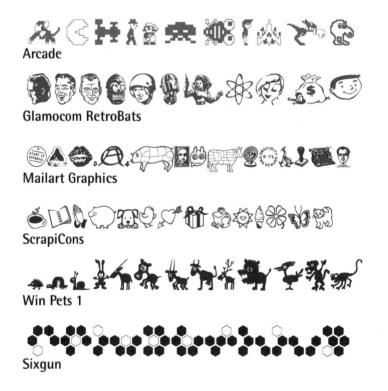

Figure 4.24: A few examples of free dingbat fonts

Finding Fonts

I've mentioned that you can find fonts on the Web a few times now, but I haven't given you any resources! Now that I've explained all six of the basic font categories, I guess it's about time to tell you where you might find some new ones to add to your typographic tool belt.

Free and Shareware Font Galleries

These web sites list and categorize thousands of free and shareware fonts from many different designers. Some of the designers listed on these galleries have their own web sites, through which they sell other fonts that they've designed. If you enjoy the fonts created by particular designers, be sure to track down the rest of their work. Many web sites claim to offer free fonts, but in my opinion these are three of the best resources:

- 1001 Fonts, at http://www.1001fonts.com/
- DaFont, at http://www.dafont.com/
- Wanted Fonts, http://www.wantedfonts.com/

Fonts for Sale

Like the free and shareware galleries mentioned above, these web sites promote fonts from many different designers and foundries. But unlike those galleries, none of these sites offer fonts for free. The benefit of paying for a font family from one of these companies is that you'll not only have a complete set of characters, but the purchased fonts often include bold, italic, oblique, and other variants.

- FontShop, at http://www.fontshop.com/
- AGFA Monotype, at http://www.fonts.com/
- Veer, at http://www.veer.com/products/type/
- MyFonts, at http://www.myfonts.com/
- International Typeface Corporation, at http://www.itcfonts.com/

Individual Artists and Foundries

Many of my favorite contemporary fonts come from a handful of individual artists and companies. Most of these web sites have a few free fonts, as well as offering a few for sale:

- **Ænigma Fonts by Brian Kent, at http://www.aenigmafonts.com/**
  Brian has developed hundreds of great free fonts. I wish his web site were easier to navigate, but it's still a great resource.
- **The Astigmatic One Eye Typographic Institute by Prof. Brian J. Bonislawsky, at http://www.astigmatic.com/**
  Professor Bonislawsky has created many terrific font faces in every imaginable category.

- **Blue Vinyl Fonts by Jess Latham, at http://www.bvfonts.com/**

  Like many font designers, Jess started designing fonts as a hobby. His freeware and paid fonts are unique and very well done.

- **Fountain by Peter Bruhn, at http://www.fountain.nu/**

  Fountain features some of the best fonts from about 20 different designers around the world. The site also provides very nice freeware fonts.

- **Larabie Fonts by Ray Larabie, at http://www.larabiefonts.com/**

  Ray is a rock star in the realm of free fonts. His work is known for having large character sets and being of very high quality.

- **Misprinted Type by Eduardo Recife, at http://www.misprintedtype.com/**

  Eduardo is the man when it comes to weathered, worn, and eclectic font faces. His work is unmistakably unique and somewhat twisted.

- **Pizzadude by Jakob Fischer, at http://www.pizzadude.dk/**

  Jacob has an admittedly goofy and laid-back style, but has cranked out over 500 handmade fonts since 1998.

Choosing the Right Fonts

Even if you understand all the technical aspects of letterforms and typeface categories, and have access to all the fonts in the world, you can still have difficulty choosing the right ones. That's because font selection is based just as heavily on artistic license and emotional association as it is on technical issues. So, where do we begin?

In order to start your quest for the perfect font, you should first define the feelings you're trying to evoke in the members of your target audience. Are you trying to show that the company the web site represents is hip and young, or would you rather portray an aura of steadfast wisdom? Do you want to create something themey, like a Luau or a Mexican fiesta, or are you trying to convey a more formal identity? By asking yourself these kinds of questions, and thinking about fonts on an emotional level, you should be able to decide reasonably easily whether a given font is appropriate for your application. If you don't think you could answer those questions about a particular font, make up your own questions. The fact is that you've probably seen billions of letters and millions of words in your lifetime—you just feel some emotional connections on which you can base your font choices. Think back to the logos, the album covers, the textbooks, and the signage you've seen. How have those typographic elements affected your perception of the entities they represent?

Now, let's take that idea and work backwards, using a generic entity like Joe's Restaurant. The font that you choose for this design will play a crucial role in the way potential diners perceive the attitude and identity of the restaurant. Take a look at Figure 4.25, and try to choose some fonts that make you think of a casual Italian bistro. Okay, now pick fonts that suggest a metropolitan restaurant serving five-star cuisine. How about a tacky dockside bar? There's no right answer for any of these scenarios, but there are definitely some fonts that just don't work in each case. First, try to narrow the field down to a few good candidates, then try to refine your choices again, until you find one that works well.

Joe's Restaurant Skia	Joe's Restaurant Versailles	*Joe's Restaurant* Legault	Joe's Restaurant Colona MT
JOE'S RESTAURANT Lithos Pro	JOE'S RESTAURANT Charlemagne	*Joe's Restaurant* Park Avenue	Joe's Restaurant Disgusting Behavior
JOE'S RESTAURANT Umbra	Joe's Restaurant Amigo	*Joe's Restaurant* Sloop	Joe's Restaurant Bubbledot ICG
Joe's Restaurant Insignia	Joe's Restaurant Adobe Jenson Pro	*Joe's Restaurant* Pelican	JOE'S RESTAURANT Cottonwood
Joe's Restaurant Bauhaus 93	Joe's Restaurant Modern No. 20	Joe's Restaurant Harrington	**joe's restaurant** Slugfest

Figure 4.25: 20 different fonts to make you want to eat at Joe's

Remember that there are no bad fonts—just inappropriate ones. While a particular font may not work for one purpose, that doesn't mean it can't be used for another. Just try to keep an open mind, and if you can narrow the field to a few possibilities, try asking a friend or coworker the question "Which one makes you feel more *adjective*?" replacing *adjective* with the feeling you're aiming to elicit.

Finally, when you're choosing fonts, it's important not to choose too many. As a rule of thumb, try not to use more than four different fonts in a web site design. Also, try to avoid combining two different serif fonts or two different sans serif fonts in the same project.

Setting Text Size

The size of text is, and always has been, a confusing topic. Over 300 years elapsed in the history of printed type before the French typefounder Père Sébastien Truchet introduced the **point**. Although points have been the standard units of measurement for typography ever since, the exact size of this "standard" unit has changed several times throughout history due to differences

between the English and French units of measurement. It wasn't until the rise of digital typography that the official size of the point was set to 1/72 inch.

While the size of type in the print world is measured by this absolute value, the size of type on the Web must be relative to the resolution of the viewer's monitor. In CSS, the pixel (**px**) is the smallest—and best—relative unit for setting the size of text. Monitor resolution is set in pixels, as are the dimensions of all display graphics, so it makes sense to control text size with pixels, as well. So, why doesn't everyone set web text sizes in pixels? Well, mainly because of Internet Explorer 6. Most browsers, including Internet Explorer, have an option that allows users to change the overall display size of the type on a web site, as Figure 4.26 shows.

Figure 4.26: **Text Size** menu in Internet Explorer

This control adds a major boost to the usability of the Web for people with visual impairments and users of low-resolution displays. In most browsers, the text size control works flawlessly, but in Internet Explorer 6, the settings in the **Text Size** menu will not affect a web page whose text is set in pixels. Why not? Because the developers of IE believe that the pixel is an absolute unit that should not be resized. Version 7 of Internet Explorer has continued the tradition of refusing to resize text set in pixels, though it does offer a page zoom feature that may constitute a good alternative for some users. Even so, setting font size in pixels cannot be recommended.

There are numerous ways to set font size, but because I think in pixels, my favorite approach involves setting a font size of ten pixels on the **body** element, and em units for the rest of the document. The default font size in most browsers is 16 pixels. And since the em is relative to the parent element's font size, the default size of one em is 16 pixels, too. So, if you wanted a page's paragraph text to display at 12 pixels, you'd have to set the font size of the paragraph to 0.75em; if

> **NOTE** *What's an em Again?*
>
> I gave a brief definition of ems in our discussion of alignment earlier in this chapter. An em is a relative unit of measurement; one em equals to the vertical size of an element's text.

you wanted 35-pixel **h1** headlines, you'd have to set them to 2.19em.[36]

I don't know about you, but I can't do decimal division in my head. Nor do I like having to drag out my calculator every time I want to set a font size in my CSS file. That's where the following 62.5% **body** font size trick comes in. By changing the font size of the **body** element, the value of one em essentially becomes ten pixels. This makes the math associated with using em-based font sizes a simple matter of moving a decimal point. In this scenario, 12 pixels is equal to 1.2 ems, and 35 pixels is equal to 3.5 ems:

```
body {
  font-size: 62.5%;
}
p {
  font-size: 1.2em;
}
h1 {
  font-size:3.5em;
}
```

This method allows me to have the pixel-by-pixel accuracy that I want as a designer, gives Internet Explorer 6 users the ability to resize the text as they see fit, and keeps me a safe distance from my calculator.

Using Punctuation and Special Characters

When you type text into any reasonably modern word processing program, even though your keyboard key shows that ubiquitous ASCII double quote symbol, you see nice "curly" opening and closing punctuation marks when you hit it. These special quotes can't be found on your keyboard, as the key in Figure 4.27 shows. But word processing programs understand that when you put something in quotes, you want nice left and right quotes, and it replaces the characters you typed in with the correct ones. The same goes with apostrophes. Have you ever seen an ASCII apostrophe like the one on your keyboard in a book or brochure? Of course not. What we usually see in printed material is a closing single quote. In fact, there exists a vast array of characters that aren't represented on a standard keyboard, though these characters show up on web pages and in printed material.

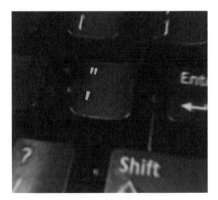

Figure 4.27: The single- and double-quote key that you see on an average keyboard

---

36   If you're wondering how I came up with those numbers, I divided the pixel size that I wanted by 16, then rounded to the nearest hundredth of an em.

Now, that's all well and good for people using word processors. But for those of us typing text into an HTML document, there's no system to automatically replace the characters from our keyboards with their grammatically correct equivalents. Depending on which type of character encoding your web site uses, when you paste these characters directly into an HTML document, you may see a bunch of gibberish on the rendered page. Also, the inclusion in text of characters that are used by HTML, like < and >, will wreak havoc in your page, as they cause the beginning or ending of HTML code.

For these reasons, a series of special codes or entities has been created—we type these into our HTML documents to produce correct punctuation marks and just about any special character that we could need. The examples in Table 4.1 are just a sample of the many HTML character codes that exist. The code on the far left is known as an **entity name** or **keyword**. For instance, to produce a copyright symbol in your document, enter **copy** directly into your HTML; you'll see a © in the rendered page. Each of these entities also has a numerical equivalent; the numerical equivalent of **copy** is **#169** which produces the same symbol. For a more complete list of codes and their alternative entity numbers, check out W3Schools' "HTML Entities" page.[37]

Table 4.1 Sample list of HTML character entity references

Entity	Character	Description
&lt;	<	Less than
&gt;	>	Greater than
&amp;	&	Ampersand
&lsquo;	'	Left single quote
&rsquo;	'	Right single quote
&ldquo;	"	Left double quote
&rdquo;	"	Right double quote
&laquo;	«	Left angle quote
&raquo;	»	Right angle quote
&reg;	®	Registered trademark
&trade;	™	Trademark
&copy;	©	Copyright
&cent;	¢	Cent
&pound;	£	Pound
&euro;	€	Euro
&yen;	¥	Yen
&frac14;	¼	One quarter
&frac12;	½	One half
&frac34;	¾	Three quarters

---

37   http://www.w3schools.com/tags/ref_entities.asp

Application: Tile Typography

By the end of the last chapter, I'd moved my boxy, colored Illustrator layout for Florida Country Tile into Photoshop, and applied texture and dimension to it. It was actually beginning to look like a real web site, as Figure 4.28 shows. As exciting as that transformation has been, it's important to get critical feedback along the way. I've communicated with the Ed the Client a few times now, getting responses about the design at each stage. Fortunately, most of his opinions thus far have been positive.

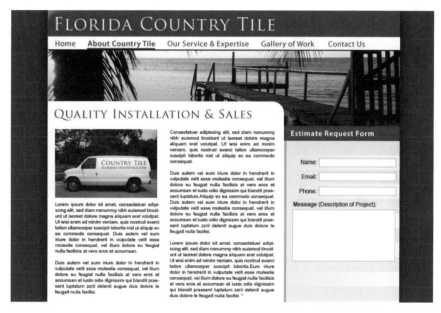

Figure 4.28: So far this design is too type-heavy for a homepage

Now that I have the basic layout approved, it's time to start chipping away at some typographic and content issues. In Chapter 1 I explained that I usually try to create some degree of contrast between the homepage and the rest of the site. Well, now is the time to get started on that. At this stage in the process, my design is still a very fluid, generic concept. The whole thing exists only in a Photoshop document, so setting up a separate homepage mockup is as easy as turning off a folder of layers and creating some new ones.

Creating the Homepage

For the sake of consistency, I generally use a homepage layout that's very similar to the layout for the rest of the site, though the homepage has a very specific task. If a web site were a brochure, the homepage would be the cover. It needs to catch the attention of viewers in a very short amount of time, and persuade them to want to delve deeper. So what could I do to make the homepage of the web site fulfill that requirement? Well, the first and most obvious solution would be to reduce the amount of text on the page. This tactic isn't going to catch the visitors' attention, though; it's only going to prevent them from feeling overwhelmed. Keeping with the brochure cover analogy, the homepage should have a singular message that's conveyed in large type.

To get started with my homepage comp, I decide to use the picture area of our layout more like a billboard than a supportive design element. I push the content blocks down to make the area larger, and combine an image of a Florida sunrise with the catchy tagline "Country Tile understands your Florida Style." On its own, this line sounds more corny than it does convincing, but with the right typographic treatment and background image, it can look elegant and sophisticated, as Figure 4.29 shows.

Figure 4.29: New billboard-style header image

What exactly did I do to make this design work? First of all, I used two different fonts from different font categories. For the first one, I stuck with Trajan Pro, the transitional serif font in which the company's logo text is set. I wanted a font that had a very personal feel for the words "Florida Style." I knew that a handwritten font was probably the way to go, but the font face Zapfino really gave the design the casual, yet elegant, look I was after. Also, by bringing in the background picture of the Florida sunrise, I was able to further contrast the two fonts, and enhance the message with some visual meaning.

Unlike a brochure, which is meant to be read in a linear way, a web site homepage is meant to be a hub from which users can jump to any content that interests them. Therefore, the little content that remains on the homepage should guide users toward some of the most popular features of the site. As a service-oriented company, the majority of Country Tile's web site visitors are going to want to know what types of work the company does, and what that work looks like. Most of this content will be found in the gallery and service sections of the web site. To help visitors get a quick answer to the question of what Country Tile actually does, I'm going to include a list of its specialties in nice large text with fancy bullets. Figure 4.30 shows how this looks.

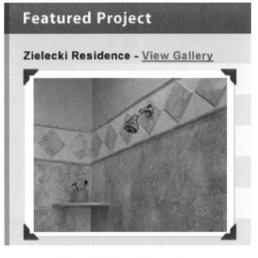

Figure 4.30: Bulleted list of Country Tile's specialties

Working on the basis that sans serif fonts are more readable than serif fonts in small body text, I plan to use a sans serif font for the main body text and the serif font Georgia for the copy headlines. Since the text of our bullet list is so large, I'm presenting the bullet text as headlines—in Georgia. Notice also that the bullets I've used in the list are images based on a character from the Wingdings dingbat font.

The other thing I really want to include on the homepage is an image link to the gallery page. To do this, I'll kick the estimate request form out of the right-hand sidebar and insert a nicely formatted thumbnail gallery link—you can see it in Figure 4.31. I've applied some photo corners to the image here; I'll apply these to the homepage using CSS backgrounds, which we'll talk about more in the next chapter. For now, though, my sidebar area now features a gallery image.

By reducing the amount of text on the page, and increasing the main area of visual interest, I've created a layout that will serve well as a homepage design for the site: as Figure 4.32 shows, it's both eye-catching and functional.

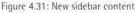

Figure 4.31: New sidebar content

The designs for the other pages of the web site will be much closer to the generic layout comp that I created earlier. However, each page will require content adjustments that help it to fulfill its specific purpose. Many of those changes will inevitably involve typographic choices like the ones we've discussed in this chapter. I'll have to make conclusive decisions about alignment, font size, and spacing. I'll need to decide if I'm going to use image text for my headlines, since they'll be relatively static, or a replacement technique like sIFR. I expect that I'll have to make more font choices, even though, at this point, I already have four fonts in my comp. I don't want to add any more fonts than that, but I'll definitely have to choose some alternate fonts for the HTML text. While these types of decisions can be made in the HTML/CSS development stage, it's best to define them early in the process, so that your client will have an accurate idea of what the finished web site will look like.

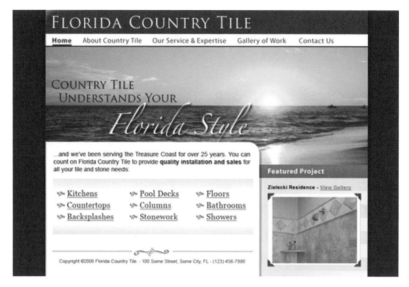

Figure 4.32: Finished homepage design for Florida Country Tile

The final chapter of the book will focus on continuing the graphic development of your web site. I'll be talking about selecting and formatting images, and making other finishing touches to the design.

CHAPTER 5

Imagery

From layout to color, from texture to type, I've been talking about imagery since the beginning of this book. So why should there be a chapter dedicated to imagery alone, right at the end? As with typography, there are many practical concerns related to imagery—including file type choices, image resolution, and photography sources—that we need to cover. But there are also artistic aspects to this topic, and these deserve some detailed discussion.

The process of choosing photographic, iconic, and illustrative elements for a web site design is a subject that requires a basic understanding of the design principles I covered in the first few chapters. Take the image above, for instance. I wanted to use an image of a camera at the top of this page as an iconic representation of the subject. However, when I was looking for a suitable picture, my decision was based more on the angle of the image than the type of camera pictured. The direction that the camera faces in this picture greatly affects the visual movement of this page. Being the only image on a page full of text instantly makes it a focal point. The direction in which your eyes move from there depends on many other factors, but most likely, they 'move' down into the first paragraph of text. If the camera were facing straight forward, the page would look just fine, but it would feel very static. If it were facing off to the right, your eye would gravitate off the page rather than down into the content. This phenomenon is due to the rules of emphasis that I talked about in Chapter 1. The placement of the camera at the top of this page helps to ensure it will get noticed. The isolation of the image makes it stand out even more as a focal point. Finally, the direction of the lens creates a line of continuance that determines the next focal point of the page.

By the end of this chapter, not only will you understand these concepts, you'll be in a solid position to apply them to your own designs.

What to Look For

The old adage that a picture is worth a thousand words certainly holds true on the Web. Photographs and illustrations often serve as visual lures that catch passing visitors and reel them into the content. On the other hand, the wrong images, or even a poor presentation of the right ones, can be detrimental to a web site's appeal. Every viewer of a photograph or illustration sees that image differently depending on his or her background and personal experience. In other words, the thousand words that one person gets out of an image may be very different from the thousand words another person gains from it.

Before you choose an image to include in the layout or the content of a web site, ask yourself the following questions:

■ **Is it relevant?**

Relevant images can add interest to your layout and enhance the content of a web page. When relevant images are placed within a block of text, they provide visual bookmarks that help visitors to remember what was covered on the page, and to know where to look when they come back. This is a very logical rule, and most people get this right when they choose images for content. However, relevance isn't the only factor to consider when choosing an image.

■ **Is it interesting?**

Although it's important to maintain a connection between the visual elements of a design and the content, this shouldn't always be priority number one. Sometimes, relevance takes a back seat to interest or intrigue. News writers often take this perspective when writing headlines for featured articles, but it can be done with images as well.

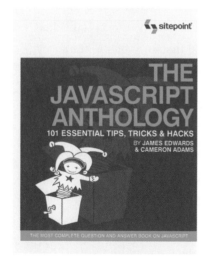

Figure 5.1: *The JavaScript Anthology* jack-in-the-box

The cover art for SitePoint's *The JavaScript Anthology*, shown in Figure 5.1, is a great example. You might ask yourself what a jack-in-the-box has to do with a JavaScript book. In a literal sense, it has very little to do with the topic, but it's an interesting and memorable image that begs for further investigation. When I think about some of the most common JavaScript applications (drop-down menus, form validation, animated transitions, and so on), I start to see the connection. A jack-in-the-box and JavaScript are about user interaction. Both usually rely on an action in order to generate a reaction, and both make life a little more interesting. I know, the connection is a little obscure, but it's there. This is what I mean when I ask if an image you're considering is interesting: does it catch your eye and make you want to understand why it's there?

■ Is it appealing?

Images that are aesthetically or emotionally appealing can be a very efficient hook for attention and emphasis. The problem is that everyone has a different definition of "appealing." The idea is to try to put yourself in the shoes of your target audience. Generally, I wouldn't design a web site that features unicorns and emeralds as design elements, but given the right target audience, that may be a valid design direction.

For every image you choose for a design, you need to be able to answer "yes" to at least two of the questions above. Why not all three? Well, sometimes it's fun to toss in an appealing and interesting image that has nothing to do with your content.

Jeffrey Zeldman does exactly this on his personal web site, zeldman.com, shown in Figure 5.2.[1] He's selected a set of images that load randomly into the photographic header area of his site. Each image is completely different and none of them seem to have any relevance to the content, or to each other. While I don't recommend this approach to image selection for corporate web sites, it does provides a unique opportunity for your site visitors to make their own creative image-to-content correlations.

Figure 5.2: Jeffrey Zeldman's web site—the random header images are interesting and appealing, but rarely relevant

---

1   http://zeldman.com/

Legitimate Image Sources

You basically have three options for coming up with images to use in the design and content of your sites:

- Do it yourself.
- Purchase stock images.
- Hire a professional.

The approach you take will depend on the budget and needs of your client.

Take It or Make It

For me, taking pictures with my own camera or creating my own illustrations is usually a win-win situation. If local clients need pictures to use on their web sites, it gives me a chance to get out of the office and do something different for a change. I've had the opportunity to take pictures of products, restaurants, a factory, apartments, a martial arts studio, storefronts—I even got to ride around on a golf cart to take pictures of a golf course one morning, all while I was on the clock. But this isn't just fun for me. Clients usually like the idea because it shows them that I want to be involved in every step of the project. It can also cost them less than it would to contract a professional photographer.

The same is usually true for illustration and animation work. Most of the time, a custom web site design requires some level of illustration. For things like icons, buttons, backgrounds, basic drawings, and logos, I'll often take a stab at fulfilling the clients' needs myself. Occasionally, this scenario doesn't work out. The illustration work they need might be outside my skill set or may be too complex for me to feel confident to take on myself. If it's a particular photo the clients want, I might not have access to the subject, or the quality of the image they need may be beyond the capabilities of my equipment. In those cases, my first instinct, and the next best option, is to turn to stock photography and illustration.

Stock Photography

If you don't have the time or ability to create or commission your own images, chances are that you can find what you're looking for in a **stock photo archive**. These photo archives, or image banks, consist of photographs and illustrations that are created for general use, rather than a specific client or project. For a licensing fee (or sometimes for free), you can select any of these images for use in your project.

Finding the right images and photos for a design project can be a difficult task, depending on two factors: the subject matter and your budget. If your project requires pictures of animals, scenic vacation destinations, office supplies, or some random inanimate object, then you're likely to have no problems finding what you're looking for. Every stock photo archive has these types of subjects well covered. Finding photos of people can be a little trickier because most stock photo sites require that the photographer submit a signed model release for any image that includes a person's face. Many people are understandably squeamish about the idea of their faces being plastered on someone's web site. Even those who aren't might be a little leery about having their pictures available for use in the public domain. For these reasons you should expect to pay for good "people pictures." Finally, if you need pictures of a product logo, a current celebrity, or some famous work of art, you've got some work to do. Even though you may be able to find these types of images easily on search engines, using them for a professional project will likely require a very detailed licensing agreement.

The next question you must answer before you begin your quest for the perfect stock image is: how much are you willing to pay? The price of using a single stock photograph can range from free to hundreds of dollars. As you can probably imagine, the average quality of free images is dramatically lower than those you'd pay for. This doesn't mean you should give up on free images altogether, though; it just means that you might have to wade through a bunch of crummy pictures before you find what you're after. The same goes for expensive images. Just because you're willing to pay $500 for a single photo doesn't mean that you're going to get a Ferrari instead of a 1970s Ford Pinto station wagon. No matter what the licensing price of an image is, it all boils down to finding what you're looking for. If you can find that quickly and at a great price, you'll have more time to spend on the design.

Three tiers of stock photography are available: free, royalty-free, and rights-managed. Let's look at each of these tiers now.

Free Images

I'm sure you've heard the saying, "there's no such thing as a free lunch." That idiom could be applied to just about everything, and it definitely applies to the world of stock photography. Even though there are some really great free stock images available, somebody is paying for the equipment and the time it takes to create those

> **WARNING   Always Look for Image Usage Guidelines**
>
> Even if an image is restriction-free, you should make sure that your use of the image falls within the guidelines of the site's image licensing agreement. On Stock.XCHNG, this information can be found underneath your chosen photo on that photo's page. Every stock photography source has different guidelines, so be sure you know what these are before you start looking for images. Some galleries even restrict the usage of their images to personal and non-profit use.

images. Why would photographers do all this for free? For the same reason a talented musician might publish free MP3s, or a team of programmers might spend time on an open-source project. It's what they love to do, it allows many more people to enjoy their work, and it's an opportunity to get their work noticed.

Of all the free stock photography sources out there, the one with the largest collection of free images, and the one that I use most often, is Stock.XCHNG, pictured in Figure 5.3.[2]

Figure 5.3: Stock.XCHNG—a quick search for "stapler" returns more than 60 images

Stock.XCHNG has over 250,000 high-quality, user-submitted images, with more being added every day. To ensure the quality and relevance of the gallery's database, site moderators check each submission before it becomes available. Stock.XCHNG also boasts an active user forum, and community members regularly publish helpful blog entries and tutorials on the site. When you're downloading images from Stock.XCHNG, be sure to check the restriction status of the image. Most images in the database are restriction-free, which means that you can use them for most personal or commercial uses.

Another great source for free stock images is MorgueFile.[3] While the user interface of MorgueFile isn't quite as quick and streamlined as Stock.XCHNG, it too has a vast collection of great images, and you're not required to register in order to download the high-resolution images. The size of any stock photography collection plays a big role in how useful it can be. Although there are many other great free stock photo resources

2   http://www.sxc.hu/
3   http://morguefile.com/

online, most of them have significantly fewer images than the sites I've mentioned here, or the images they offer cover only very specific topics.

If you've spent any time looking for the right free stock image, you'll know that finding what you need can be a frustrating experience. Sometimes you'll waste more time searching than designing, and when it's a client project you're working on, you simply can't afford to waste time. When you're willing to pay a little for the right image, the task of finding that image becomes much easier. That's when paid stock images, which generally come in two flavors—royalty-free and rights-managed—come to the fore.

Royalty-free Images

Contrary to what you might think, a **royalty-free** image is not available for use free of charge. The term refers to the details of the image's licensing agreement. A royalty-free image license is one that allows you to pay a single, up-front fee for an image. The payment buys you the right to use that image for other clients and projects without paying further licensing fees, known as royalties. As you can imagine, this is a popular option with designers who may need the same types of images again and again, and don't want to deal with the hassle of negotiating usage rights.

Before high-speed Internet was widely available, royalty-free images came mainly in the form of CD collections. Rather than purchasing the right to an individual image, a designer would purchase a CD collection that had many images with the same theme, subject, or style. While this is still a popular option for large companies that complete a lot of design work, the prices of these types of CDs can be prohibitively expensive for a freelance designer or small firm. These days, the option of browsing stock photo galleries online and purchasing the rights to use individual images has become more practical, and sometimes more affordable, than purchasing entire CDs of stock images. One of the fastest growing and most popular places to purchase royalty-free stock photography is iStockphoto, shown in Figure 5.4.[4]

While many of the larger stock photo sources, like Corbis,[5] Getty Images,[6] and Jupiterimages,[7] only source content from professional photographers, iStockphoto makes it easy for anyone to submit their own images and artwork. To maintain the quality and diversity of the iStockphoto collection, the site administrators accept only high-quality images and often reject subjects on which they already have an abundance of imagery.

---

4   http://www.istockphoto.com/
5   http://www.corbis.com/
6   http://www.gettyimages.com/
7   http://www.jupiterimages.com/

Figure 5.4: iStockphoto—with over a million indexed photos, iStockphoto is likely to have what you're after

The difference in quality between Stock.XCHNG and iStockphoto is quite simple: iStockphoto pays its photographers. Therefore, the site attracts more submissions of higher quality. Purchasing images here is based on a credit system. Once you've created an account, you can purchase a pack of credits, which is sort of like buying tickets for a carnival. The minimum credit package is $10 for ten credits. The lower-resolution images on iStockphoto are usually all you really need for web design, and cost one credit each. So essentially, each of these low-resolution images is only $1. Another source of low-cost, royalty-free images is Dreamstime.[8] Although Dreamstime has roughly half the images that iStockphoto has, it's quickly gaining popularity and a strong reputation in the design community.

If you plan to download a lot of stock photography, paying by the image can become expensive, even at $1 apiece. An alternative to the credit-based system is to pay for a subscription service. A few stock photography providers do not sell images individually; rather, they charge a monthly subscription fee that allows you to download whatever you need. Two such providers are Photos.com[9] and Shutterstock.[10] Although these types of services start at around $140 per month, they offer discounts for customers who purchase multiple months' access at a time—that might make it worth your while!

Rights-managed Images

A third level of stock photography service is known as **rights-managed**. This type of stock photography can be quite a bit pricier than the others, as you pay a fee based on the size

---

8   http://www.dreamstime.com/
9   http://www.photos.com/
10   http://www.shutterstock.com/

of your business, the number of people that will be exposed to the image, and the amount of time for which the image will be in use. The photos in a rights-managed collection are usually of an extremely high quality. Also, because the company in charge of the rights knows who's using them, and for how long, incidents in which your client's competitor has on its homepage the exact same image you've used on your client's homepage are highly unlikely.

With such a large pool of royalty-free images available, it may already seem unlikely, but this is precisely what happened to Dell and Gateway in the summer of 2004. Both computer manufacturers were embarrassed when they featured photos of the same college girl on their homepages at the same time. While shelling out extra money for rights-managed photography may help your clients to avoid this type of scenario, exclusivity is not guaranteed. If you need to ensure that a picture that you use on a web site won't be used by anyone else, the best option is to have photos taken professionally.

Getting Professional Help

If you plan to hire a professional photographer to do your dirty work, be sure to find one that has experience with commercial photography and the type of shots you're looking for. That excellent photographer who captured your brother-in-law's tears at a cousin's wedding, for instance, may be great at portraiture and event shots, but he might not know the first thing about architectural or product photography.

The best way to find a good commercial photographer is by word of mouth. If you know of other companies that have hired a professional photographer, ask them about their photographers and the experience. If you don't have any references that you can ask, try starting with a local professional association. If you're in the US, the Advertising Photographers of America web site is a great place to start.[11] Many of the photographers listed in the APA database have biographies and portfolios that can give you a good idea of their capabilities.

To ensure that you have an accurate handle on the costs, be very specific when writing a request for proposal. Be sure to include the details of each shot you need. State where you'd like to have the pictures taken if they're going to be done outside the photographer's studio, and be ready (with models, locations, wardrobes, etc.) to take all the pictures on the same day if possible. Most professional photographers charge by the day or half-day. Daily rates can vary quite a bit, depending on the market and the photographer's experience, but they can range from just under one thousand to several thousand dollars. Another thing to take into consideration is the photographer's copyright and usage guidelines. Many photographers will grant full ownership of the original photographs to your client upon payment. Some will require credit if the work is used in a commercial publication. A few

---

11   http://www.apanational.com/

photographers may require that they retain exclusive rights to the pictures they take, and they'll charge per use of the photos. You should try to negotiate full ownership and usage permissions whenever possible, but keep in mind that this type of contract may cost more.

No matter what sources you use for your images—whether you get them from a free stock web site like Stock.XCHNG, or pay a professional photographer to take them—it will ultimately be your clients who should have the final say. Even though it will likely be your job to choose the images that you feel best represent their companies, sometimes your clients might not agree with your choices. Always be ready to fall back and make changes where necessary. As long as you're creating good work and getting your images from legitimate sources, your hard work should pay off, and the clients will be impressed.

How Not to Impress

So I've told you about a few legitimate means by which you can obtain imagery for your projects. Now it's time to talk about where *not* to get imagery from. I'm confident that by now you know enough about layout, color, texture, and typography to figure out how to use images in your designs, but what if you don't have any images to work with?

Sometimes, clients will have sets of images that they would like to see used on their web sites. Sometimes, they know at least which *types* of pictures they want on which pages. Quite often, though, coming up with layout and content images will fall on your shoulders as the designer. If this is the case, here are a few image sources that you should avoid.

Google Ganking

As a web designer, you may find it inspirational to run a Google or Flickr image search for topics around which you're building a web site. Let's say you're building a web site for a bike shop. If the owner of the shop hasn't given you any images to work with yet, doing an image search for mountain biking, bike races, road bikes, and other related subjects can give you a better visual understanding of the topic, and an idea about the types of images

Okay, so the penalties of stealing images probably don't involve handcuffs, but don't do it!

you'll want to use on the site. Usually, this type of search will return some images that would work well in your design. You might even feel the urge to save some of these images to your computer, open them up in Photoshop and crop, resize, and modify them a little to fit your needs. This is known as **Google Ganking**, and it's a serious problem in web design. Unless the images on a web site are specifically marked as being free to use or available in the public domain, you can assume that they are copyrighted by the site's owner, and therefore you'll need permission to use them. You may think the image's owner will never notice your rip of his or her work, but you run the risk of enduring something as embarrassing as having a cease and desist letter sent to your client, or something as serious as a lawsuit.

Even if an image is clearly marked as being free to use, it's always nice to let the creator know how and where you plan to use his or her work.

Hotlinking

If there's anything that designers hate more than seeing their designs or images ripped off, it's seeing them ripped off by a site that's linking to the files on the designers' own servers. Usually, images for a web site are placed on the same web server as the site, and are linked to in the way shown here:

```
<img src="/images/image.jpg" height="150" width="100" alt="Image" />
```

However, images can also be linked to from outside the web site, using the full URL of the image:

```
<img src="http://www.somesite.com/images/image.jpg" height="150" width="100"
    alt="Image" />
```

Going back to my theoretical bike shop example, let's suppose I wanted to use a picture of a particular make and model of bike. Let's say I found an image of the right bike on the manufacturer's site and wanted to use it. Rather than requesting product images from the manufacturer, or even downloading the image and placing it on my client's web server, let's imagine I decide to link straight to the image on the bike manufacturer's web site. This dubious practice is called **hotlinking**.

Copyright issues aside, hotlinking uses the bandwidth of the web site on which the images are located. With most hosting accounts, bandwidth is limited and extra bandwidth can be expensive. As a real-world metaphor, hotlinking is a little bit like using someone else's cellphone minutes to make your call. Most web professionals know that hotlinking is a big faux pas, so the usual hotlinking suspects are forum users, bloggers, and MySpace users who don't know any better. If you didn't before, now you know better, too.

Clipart

Many web sites offer free, or very cheap, clipart and illustration packages. While these cheesy, generic graphics may work for an internal company bulletin, or a corny do-it-yourself greeting card, they should be considered off-limits for any professional project.

You may think that I'm being a little harsh with that statement, but take a moment to think about it. If you go to a five-star restaurant, would you expect to be served instant mashed potatoes from a box? Of course not! You would expect fresh ingredients, cooked from scratch. As a designer, you have an obligation to cook something up for your client that is

Clipart could make this happen to YOU.

as original as it is astonishing. While the quality and "freshness" of stock photography can be questionable as well, there's nothing worse than seeing a good design blemished by stale, clichéd clipart. If your client asks you to use clipart or a cheesy animated GIF on the site, you should push back a little. Just remember that if the client has come to you for the design, it's your job to provide feedback that will make it look good. However, you also have to remember that the client is always right. Sometimes a client will force a design decision, and you'll just have to go with it. I guess some people just really like their instant potatoes.

Regardless of how good a job you've done choosing images for your design, there's another critical factor to consider: presentation. When you're formatting images for use on your site, their presentation will often depend on the constraints of the layout you've chosen. The image size, for instance, may depend on the size of the rectangle you have available in your grid. As the designer, it's up to you to determine how an image will be cropped, if it will have any framing or borders, and what types of visual effects will be applied to the image, if any.

Creative Cropping

Some of the most profound impacts you can make on the presentation of an image come from wise choices about what should be included, and what should not. This process is known as **cropping**, and is a fundamental image manipulation technique.

At its most basic level, cropping can be used to eliminate unnecessary or unsightly details from a picture. The picture in Figure 5.5 is one that I took while wandering around with my wife in downtown Charleston, South Carolina. It's an okay picture, but

Figure 5.5: An unedited photo of downtown Charleston

the people in the immediate foreground and the power lines that run down the shady right-hand side of the street are distracting.

By cutting off some of the bottom and the right side of the photo, the entire image—shown in Figure 5.6—feels much more casual and less busy. In the original photo, the perspective made the church steeple the focal point, but the image included too many other things that competed with it for viewers' attention. After I crop the shot, the steeple is still the focal point, but the pair of shoppers jumps out as a secondary focal point. Even though the steeple isn't in the center of the composition, the perspective lines that run along the top of the buildings, the edge of the road, and even the yellow line, point toward the steeple's base. Having this off-center element as the focal point of the image creates a more interesting composition and helps to give the image a more intentional feel.

Figure 5.6: Charleston cropped

We can also crop images in unexpected ways to portray a sense of emotion, show an interesting perspective, or change the overall message of the image. In Figure 5.7, an image of a guitar player has been cropped in tightly to show only the musician's strumming hand and the body of the guitar. This treatment highlights the sense of movement that's inherent in a musical performance, and provides a degree of anonymity that allows more people to connect with the image.

Figure 5.7: Tight cropping to give an image a sense of emotion and movement

When cropping images tightly, as I did with the guitar image, it's important to be aware of the overall size of the image you're working with. You may want to crop to and enlarge a particular, very detailed area of the photo, but if the image's resolution is too low, the cropped image may look pixelated. Fortunately, images that are used on the Web can have much lower resolutions than those used in print, but always check the quality of your final image to make sure that it isn't grainy or blurry.

Images don't always have to be contained in boxes. Many of the fun and useful ways in which we can crop photos are more creative than just trimming off the sides. The photo in Figure 5.8 is one that I took from the banks of the Saluda River, South Carolina. I love this

Figure 5.8: The Saluda River

picture so much in its unedited form that I made it into a background image for my computer, but let's try to think outside the box.

Unconventional cropping methods can come off as amateurish if they're poorly executed, but if they're done well, they can be used to create some very striking graphics. Let's say I was designing a web site for an outdoor center that rented kayaks for use on the Saluda River. In that case, I might use a technique like the one illustrated in Figure 5.9.

Figure 5.9: River image cropped around a kayaking shape

Here, I've used a vector image of a pair of kayakers as a mask around which to crop my original Saluda River picture. In image editing software, a mask is basically a window through which you can see the image. When I laid the mask of the kayakers over the image of the river, I got the top half of Figure 5.9. By flipping the mask vertically, and applying it to a blue-tinted duplicate of the original, I was able to create the appearance of a reflection.

Now that image might work for a kayak rental center web site, but what if we were creating images for a web site that promoted a regional visitor's center? A visitor's center wouldn't want to impose the idea that the river is only great for kayaking. It's also a great area for swimming, hiking, and fishing. By using the text "RIVER" as a mask in Figure 5.10, I've made the image much more versatile, while establishing a fresh and creative look.

Figure 5.10: Using text as a mask to crop the Saluda River image

One final non-rectangular approach to cropping involves removing an image entirely from a scene. The part of the image that we remove is known as a **knock out**. A knocked out image can be featured without a background, placed onto another image, or even duplicated and rotated several times to make a flower. Okay, so maybe the last example of using a knock out in Figure 5.11 is a bit far-fetched, but you have to admit that my banana flower looks pretty darn cool.

Figure 5.11: Examples of knock outs—a background-less bunch of bananas, a bunch of bananas in the sky, and a banana flower

As you can see, cropping provides endless possibilities for the production of unique images and design elements. The only limiting factors are your imagination and your ability to flesh out ideas in Photoshop.

Photoshop Adjustments

While many software packages are available to help us edit images, Adobe Photoshop has long been my tool of choice. Despite its steep price tag and learning curve, my workflow would suffer without it. It's the genuine Swiss Army knife of image editing software packages, and is the undisputed industry standard. Other tools may be cheaper, but they only have the knife, or the nail file, or maybe just the cheap plastic toothpick. Photoshop, on the other hand, slices, dices, and creates convincing watercolor painting-styled images in milliseconds. However, even though I'll refer to Photoshop quite often in the following discussion, most of the topics I'm going to talk about here are basic image adjustments that come standard (in some form or another) with just about every image editing software on offer. I guess what I'm saying is that this section is really about image adjustments, or "photoshopping" with a lowercase "p."

When I'm taking personal pictures with my digital camera, I usually try to think a little about each shot's composition and lighting, but I'm not really a photography pro, so my photos generally don't turn out so great. Those "not so great" images often go straight to my personal photo gallery as records of places or events. If I'm taking a picture for a design project, though, there's rarely a time when that image doesn't undergo some major changes before it's suitable for use in client work. At a minimum, the changes I'll make usually include cropping, and altering the brightness, contrast, and saturation of the photo.

Figure 5.12: Another raw photo—the entrance of the Biltmore Estate

Figure 5.12 is an example of a photo straight from my digital camera. It's a picture of the amazing stonework around the entrance to the Biltmore Estate in Asheville, North Carolina, that I took during a visit last summer. It's an okay photograph, but it's definitely not fit for professional use. Even as a straight content image, it has competing focal points and feels unbalanced.

Figure 5.13: Initial cropping of Biltmore entrance carving

My first step is usually to crop the image to focus on the aspects I want to show. In this case, I plan to highlight the human figure to the right of the door. As a hypothetical scenario, let's say I want to use it for the feature image in a news article about the Biltmore Estate. I like the close-up of the sculpture in Figure 5.13, but I want to find a creative way to hide the "rooftop" over its head. One way I could achieve this would be to use an image box that cuts off the rooftop element, but shows the figure popping out of the top and left-hand sides. Figure 5.14 shows how the finished effect would look.

To create this effect in Photoshop, I need two image layers: one that has the isolated stone figure, and another that has the background. I start out by duplicating my image several times, making sure to keep one completely unedited version in case I need to go back to step one. For the top layer, I carefully knocked out the figure by zooming in and using the Polygonal Lasso tool to select the perimeter of the figure and cut off the excess. To create the background image, I used the rounded rectangle tool to create a mask of the area I wanted to show, then dragged the mask onto my background box layer.

Figure 5.14: The Biltmore image double-cropped with two layers

The resulting image looks pretty good, but it could still use some adjustments. The first issue I have is that the grimy areas on the figure's shoulders and shield are a bit unsightly. I'm not going to eliminate that completely, but I can take some steps to reduce the contrast in those areas. The tools for this job are the Dodge and Burn tools. The Dodge tool is a brush-like tool that actually lightens the area that you click on, while the Burn tool darkens the area. By using these tools together, I can lighten the dark areas, and darken the light areas, to give the image more consistent shading and contrast.

Next, it's time to adjust the overall brightness and contrast of the two layers. Brightness and Contrast are two controls that are provided by just about every image editing software; they can be accessed in the Photoshop menu through the **Image** > **Adjustments** > **Brightness/ Contrast...** menu options. The controls are shown in Figure 5.15.

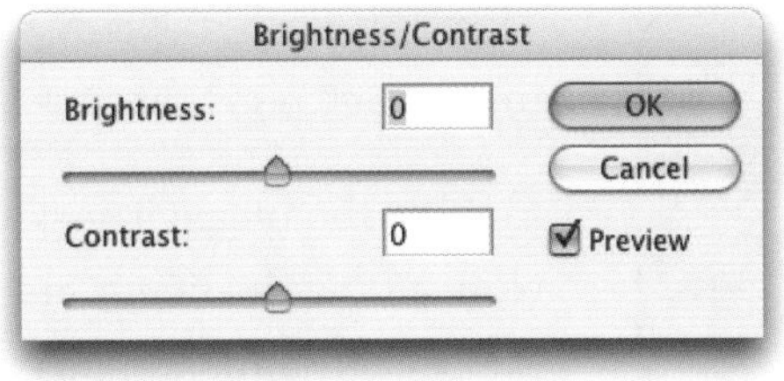

Figure 5.15: Photoshop's Brightness/Contrast controls

The **brightness** of an image actually refers to the overall amount of light or darkness in the image. The **contrast** of an image is the difference between the light and dark areas of the image. Kicking the brightness and contrast of the Biltmore figure up a few notches, and pushing the brightness and contrast of the background block down a bit, will help to give the composition a little more pop.

After I adjust the brightness and contrast, I move on to work on the hue and saturation. You can access the Hue and Saturation controller shown in Figure 5.16 can be accessed through the **Image** > **Adjustments** > **Hue/Saturation…** menu options.

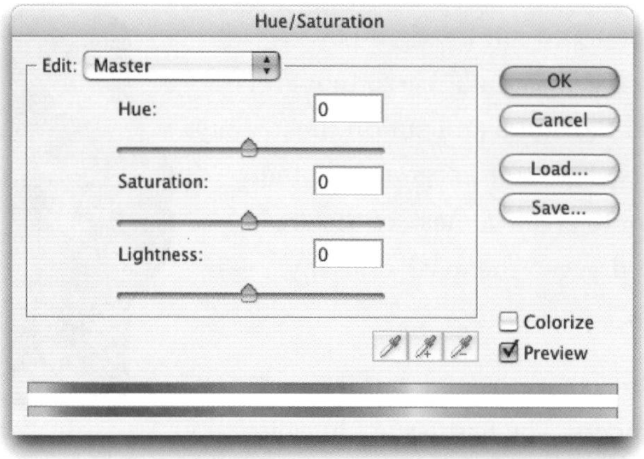

Figure 5.16: Photoshop Hue/Saturation controls

The **Hue** control affects the overall color of the image. By moving the **Hue** slider up and down, you can shift all the colors in the image so that it appears more blue, or red, or orange, and so on. The overall tone of this image is fine, so I don't really want to adjust its hue too much, but it's sometimes necessary to alter the hue if you want to change the overall color of an image. The **Saturation** slider affects how saturated the colors appear within the image. If you turn the saturation off, you'll be left with a grayscale image, but if you turn it all the way up, all the colors will be brighter and more dramatic. I want to increase the saturation in the image of the figure, and reduce the saturation of the background image. This will further extenuate the contrast, and give the image the "pop" that I was talking about before.

Finally, the image is just about ready for posting! Notice how the figure in Figure 5.17 stands out from the background, and has much more even shading than it did before. These subtle details make a big difference in the overall effect of the image. To adjust a little more of that detail, I applied an outline stroke around the background block by accessing **Layer** > **Layer Style** > **Stroke…** and giving the block an inside black stroke.

Figure 5.17: Final image after Photoshop tweaking

Besides making brightness, contrast, and saturation adjustments, another way to give an image a Photoshop facelift is through the use of **filters**.

In photography, a filter is a physical attachment for your camera lens that alters the way a photo looks. These filters are used to capture richer colors, compensate for bad lighting, or make an image feel warmer or cooler. Photoshop filters follow this basic idea, though they do much more than a camera lens attachment. They can be used to create artistic effects, distort images, add texture, and much more. Photoshop comes stocked with a great variety of filters as Figure 5.18 shows. Some of these can be very useful, and some … well, I don't find them so useful, but suffice it to say that there's something for everyone. Just to get an idea of what's possible with filters, I opened a picture of some orchids and ran it through a few of the standard filters in Photoshop. Figure 5.19 shows the results of my experiment.

Figure 5.18: Photoshop's Artistic filters

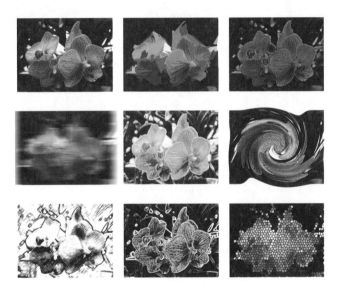

Figure 5.19: A sampling of some of Photoshop's filters

As far as Photoshop effects go, I've really only shown the tip of the iceberg here. Not even the whole tip—this quick tour has been more like a chip off the tip. There is so much that you can do within Photoshop, and my best recommendation for learning it all is to tinker. Online tutorials and instructional books like SitePoint's *The Photoshop Anthology* will accelerate that process, but there's no substitute for solid experience.[12] Open an image and just start to explore what each toolbar button, drop-down item, menu action, and filter can do to that image. Once you've messed up that image pretty well, open another one and start again.

---

12   http://www.sitepoint.com/books/photoshop1/

File Formats and Resolutions

No matter which photo editing program you use, to prepare images for the Web you'll need to know a few basics about the standard image file formats and when each should be used. Currently, three image formats are widely supported by web browsers:

■ **JPEG**

The JPEG format is an image compression format that was developed by the Joint Photographic Experts Group specifically to store photographic images. Although there's no limit to the number of colors the JPEG format can display, it's a lossy format that can create visual artifacts depending on how much you compress the file—see Figure 5.20.

Figure 5.20: An image of a strawberry saved at increasing levels of JPEG compression

■ **GIF**

GIF (Graphics Interchange Format) is an eight-bit format that compresses files on the basis of the number of colors in the image. Although the compression ratio of the GIF format is very good, it supports a maximum of only 256 colors and is therefore useless for photographs. However, the format is suitable for images that contain very few colors, or large blocks of solid color. Images such as logos, cartoons, and line drawings are great candidates for being saved as GIFs. Two other nifty features of GIF are that it can display transparency (see Figure 5.21), and it supports animation. In the late 1990s, UNYSIS (the company behind the compression algorithm used in GIF images) tried to claim that GIF was a proprietary format, and charged companies royalties for any program that created GIF files. This, and the 256 color limitation of the format, led to the creation of the PNG format.

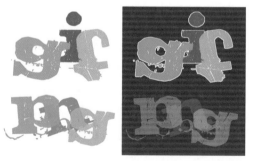

Figure 5.21: A transparent GIF and a transparent PNG shown against different backgrounds

■ **PNG**

The PNG (Portable Networks Graphics) format was developed by the W3C as an alternative to GIF. The lossless compression style of the PNG algorithm works similarly to that of GIF in that files with fewer colors end up having the smallest file sizes. Like GIF, PNG also supports transparency, though it does it so much better than GIF. With GIF images, transparency is binary: it's either on or off. Transparency in PNG images is implemented by means of an **alpha channel** that sits alongside the red, green, and blue channels, meaning that each pixel in a PNG image can have up to 256 different levels of opacity. The effects of this difference are illustrated in Figure 5.21—notice that you can still see the background image through the PNG image, while the GIF is either completely opaque or completely transparent. Unfortunately, Internet Explorer 6 does not support transparency in PNG images properly, though Internet Explorer 7 does.

Borders and Edge Treatments

Once you have inserted your JPEG, PNG, or GIF image into your web page, you may still find yourself a bit underwhelmed by its presentation. By default, images that are placed on a web page using an HTML **<img>** tag sit inline with the text that surrounds them. A hyperlinked image typically has a rather unattractive blue border. But what if you want to give an image a frame like one you might use to display a picture on your wall? What if you want an image to have a border around it that makes it look like a Polaroid picture? Perhaps you want it to have corner tabs like the ones you'd use to stick an image into a photo book. In these cases, you have two options: apply your desired effects directly to the photo using image editing software, or use CSS background images and borders to style the image within your web page. You can see my creative use of a border in Figure 5.22.

Figure 5.22: My 2¢ on adding edge and border effects to images

Applying Effects Directly to the Image

Altering an image to add borders and edging effects may not seem like a big hassle. It only takes a little quality time with Photoshop to give a photo the look you want. But problems can arise if you have to give every image on a web site the same look. And what would happen if you had to add new images or change any of the existing pics? In either case, a task that would normally involve only a minor change to your HTML, plus a second or two to copy the new photo to the web server, might take half an hour or more. On top of that, the whole point of semantic markup is to separate style from content. An image in the content of a web site is just that: content. For those reasons, most standards-lovin' designers try to apply image styling—especially edge effects—via CSS, rather than to the image itself.

That said, there are still times when Photoshopping edge effects onto an image is worth it; sometimes, the decision is dictated by the amount of effort you'd need to expend to create the same effect using background images and CSS. Take a look at the grid image in Figure 5.23, which is taken from the Building Maintenance Service's web site.[13]

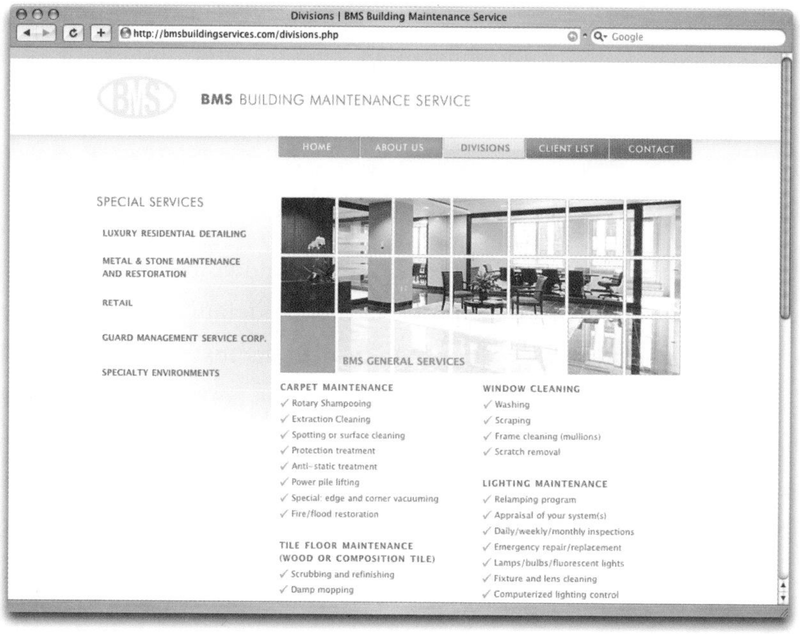

Figure 5.23: Building Maintenance Service's web site—the photo grid is a single image, with the grid overlay applied directly to the image itself

Separating a large image into a grid of smaller ones gives this page of the Building Maintenance Service's web site a very clean, modern feel. Each of the image segments within the grid has a one-pixel, gray border that gives the overall composition some dimension, and ties it to the site's color scheme. While recreating this effect as a series of images with CSS borders is possible, it's totally impractical and would add a ton of unnecessary HTML and CSS to the site. On the other hand, creating the grid that overlays this image in Photoshop is quick and easy, and if the client ever wanted to swap the image, it would be a simple matter of placing the new image on a new layer beneath the grid layer, and saving the resulting image.

---

13 http://bmsbuildingservices.com/divisions.php

Since I kept handy the Photoshop file for the little 2¢ stamp image that I made for Figure 5.22, adding that border to another photo using Photoshop would be just as easy as changing the image for the Building Maintenance Service's site. While the stamp border looks complicated and intricate, it really didn't take long to create. Here are the steps I took, in case you'd like to create a perforated stamp-style border like this yourself:

1 Using the Rectangle tool, create a rectangle that's about the size you want your stamp to be. It doesn't matter what color this rectangle is, as long as it's not the same color as the background. I made mine a particularly jarring teal, just to prove that it didn't matter.

2 Using the Ellipse tool, hold down the *Shift* key and create a small circle on the bottom-left edge of your rectangle. By holding down the *Shift* key, you're forcing the tool to make a circle, rather than allowing you to make an oval. Change the color of this circle to something other than the color of your rectangle. Since the color we use doesn't really matter, I chose purple.

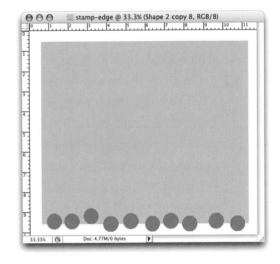

Figure 5.24: Making progress, but still ugly

3 Select the Move tool and hold down the *Alt* key (*Option* on a Mac) while dragging your image to the right. This should create a duplicate of your circle. Repeat this step until you've lined the bottom edge of your rectangle with circles. At this point, you should have something like Figure 5.24.

4 With the Move tool still selected, select all the circle layers in your layer palette. To do this, click on the top one, then hold down the *Shift* key and click the last layer. From the menu, select **Layer** > **Align** > **Vertical Centers**. Then go to **Layer** > **Distribute** > **Horizontal Centers**. This will align vertically, and space evenly, all the purple circles.

5 Rather than repeating steps 2 to 4 to create circles for the top edge of the image, simply make sure all your circle layers are still selected, hold down the *Alt* key again (*Option* on a Mac) and drag a copy of your circle row up to the top edge of the rectangle.

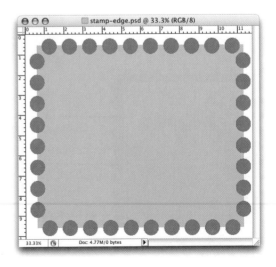

Figure 5.25: Is it making any sense yet?

6 To create more circles for the sides of your box, just hold down the *Alt* (or *Option*) key again, drag a copy of your circle row into the center of the rectangle area, and go to **Edit > Transform > Rotate 90 CW**. Move the circles around until your rectangle is completely surrounded by circles, like the one in Figure 5.24.

7 Now it's time to get rid of those horrible colors. Merge all of the layers in your image into one by selecting **Layer > Flatten Image**. Then use the Magic Wand tool to select your rectangle. This should select the area not covered by purple dots.

8 To round off the corners of the selected stamp shape a bit, bring up the **Smooth Selection** dialog by selecting **Select > Modify > Smooth…**. You may want to experiment with the value you enter into this dialog, but *5* should be a good number to start with.

9 Now hide this layer, create a new layer, and use the Paint Bucket Tool to fill the layer with a solid color.

10 To finish off this stamp-bordered rectangle, I added a little Web 2.0-style gradient and a drop shadow. With your new layer selected, go to **Layer > Layer Style > Drop Shadow…**. Choose your preferred settings, then go to **Layer > Layer Style > Gradient Overlay…** and do the same. This time I chose to go with an orange gradient rather than using blue. Figure 5.26 shows how it turned out. Notice the very subtle use of drop shadows and gradients. It's important not to overdo layer styles in Photoshop—overdone effects and filters tend to make your final images look cheap.

Figure 5.26: Final stamp-bordered image

Obviously, this type of border isn't all that versatile. It's a great conceptual piece of Photoshop border design, but it's very themey and probably won't find a use in any of my future client work. That's usually the case with custom borders and image effects that I create in Photoshop. I come up with an idea for an effect that I want to use on a particular image in a specific project, and I create the effect, but I don't use it again until I need to update that image.

Applying Effects with CSS

If I had a bunch of images to which I wanted to apply this stamp effect, and those images were all the same size, I'd probably keep the background image generic, like the one in Figure 5.26, and use CSS to add the effect. If I apply a background to an object through CSS, I'll be able to update the borders and styles of multiple images simultaneously—I won't have to edit each individual image. If a number of images on your web site are all the same size, and they change often, this approach is the one to choose if you want them to have a consistent style. As Figure 5.27 shows, the designers at 13 Strides Creative took this approach with the borders around their portfolio thumbnails.[14]

Figure 5.27: The thumbnail images on 13 Strides Creative's site display borders applied with background images and CSS

Each of these thumbnail images is wrapped in an <a> tag that has the teal border image as a background. Some padding is applied to the links, and they're floated left to form that nice grid image.

CSS Borders

Of course, not all CSS-based edge effects involve background images. CSS borders provide myriad possible effects that do not rely on extra images. As you may already know, CSS borders have three properties—width, style, and color—which are controlled individually via the **border-width**, **border-style**, and **border-color** properties, and by the shorthand **border** property. The **border-width** and **border-color** properties are fairly self-explanatory. **border-**

---

14   http://www.13strides.com/

width sets the thickness of the border by being set either to a CSS measurement (such as **1px** or **0.5em**) or a keyword (one of **thin**, **medium**, or **thick**). The **border-color** property takes a hexadecimal color value.

The **border-style** property is where the developers of CSS got their creativity on. We have eight visual styles to choose from: **dotted**, **dashed**, **solid**, **double**, **groove**, **ridge**, **inset**, and **outset**. **border-style** could also be set to **none** or **hidden**. Although **border-style** is one of my favorite CSS properties, I wish its creators had defined the details of these values a little more precisely for the browser manufacturers. As you can see in Figure 5.28, there are many subtle differences between the ways the borders display in each browser.

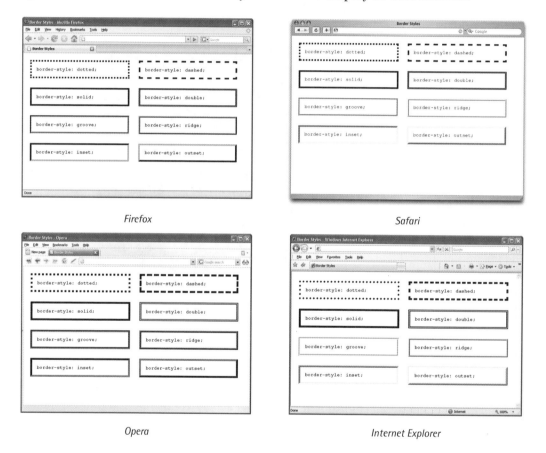

Figure 5.28: The eight visible border styles as seen in four different browsers

Even with these slight inconsistencies, each style is clearly distinguished and potentially useful. I use the word "potentially" because, depending on how they're used, these borders also have the potential to be ugly. Just as good typography exists to complement text, a good border should complement the item it surrounds. Particularly large borders, or those that have a lot of color contrast, will distract viewers from the image to which you wished to draw more attention.

You can take full advantages of borders' ugly potential by specifying completely different borders for each side of a block. The ability to specify borders separately can be extremely useful if you want to specify a border on one side of a block only, or if you want to use different colors within the same border. But mixing different styles, colors, and thickness values around the same element or image usually only leads to trouble. As you can see from the scary monkey image in Figure 5.29, this approach can produce some fairly horrific results (though I'd have to admit that the toy itself doesn't help matters).

The following CSS created the ugly box in Figure 5.29:

```
img.uglybox {
  border-top: 20px groove #ff1100;
  border-right: 16px dotted #66ee33;
  border-bottom: 8px outset #00aaff;
  border-left: 12px double #ff00ff;
}
```

Figure 5.29: CSS can produce scary borders

CSS Border Drop Shadows

Thankfully, applying different CSS border properties to a single image doesn't have to be scary. The awesome powers of borders can be used just as well for good as they can for evil. One graphic edge effect that designers often want to apply to the images in their designs is drop shadowing. In Chapter 3 I mentioned a few resources that can help us apply effects like rounded corners to HTML elements. Well, there are at least as many resources out there for creating drop shadow-like effects in CSS as there are for creating rounded corners. One very simple method for creating a tiny drop shadow involves placing a one-pixel, solid border on the bottom and right-hand sides of an element. This is what Dan Cedarholm has done to his portfolio, and thumbnail images, on the work section of his own web site, SimpleBits, shown in Figure 5.30.[15]

---

15 http://www.simplebits.com/

Figure 5.30: Teeny, tiny CSS border drop shadows at SimpleBits

Both the larger image on the left, and the smaller thumbnail images on the right, have tiny drop shadow border effects that were created using these single-pixel solid bottom and right-side borders. To add to the effect, each image is padded by a few pixels, which adds whitespace and makes each image feel more like a photograph.

Multiple Image Effects

Sometimes, when you're designing edge effects for an image or text block, you want to be able to apply the effect to objects of varying sizes. While CSS borders can handle objects of varying sizes, a border that's based on a single image cannot. In those cases, multiple images can be used to make the effect more flexible. Have a look at Figure 5.31—the photo corners that I created for my wife's and my personal site, amesnjas.com is a good example of a border that can be applied to images of varying heights.[16]

Figure 5.31: Image corners and subtle drop shadows applied using CSS

---

16   http://www.amesnjas.com/

All of the photos on amesnjas.com are managed via Zenphoto, an excellent open-source PHP- and MySQL-based image gallery application.[17] The gallery images, like the one in Figure 5.32, are resized to a given width automatically; as a result of the fact that the width is standard, the heights of the resized images can vary a lot. If all the images were one size, we could apply a background image to the link tag that already wraps the image—a technique we saw 13 Strides Creative use back in Figure 5.27. However, we need to adjust this approach when our images vary in size.

By wrapping the image link in a **<div>** tag, I was able to give both the link and the **div** separate background images. The background of the link is aligned to the bottom of the image, and the background of the **<div>** tag is aligned to the top of the image. The exploded diagram in Figure 5.32 shows how I applied the background images to each element.

Figure 5.32: Exploded diagram of top and bottom photo corners

The background of the **div** is an image that includes the two top photo corners; it's visible through the padding that's applied to the link element. The background of the link element is a similar image containing the bottom photo corners. This image is aligned to the bottom of the link element and is also visible through the padding applied to this element. The padding helps to expand the clickable area associated with the link, ensuring that it's as easy to click on as possible. When all is said and done, the HTML for this effect is fairly simple:

```
<div class="photobox">
  <a href="bigdog.jpg" title="Big Dog"><img src="dog.jpg" alt="Dog" /></a>
</div>
```

And the CSS is straightforward as well:

```css
.photobox {
  background-image: url('photobg-top.gif');
  background-position: top;
  background-repeat: no-repeat;
}
.photobox a {
  display: block;
  text-align: center;
  text-decoration: none;
  padding: 16px 0 10px 0;
  background-image: url('photobg-bot.gif');
  background-position: bottom;
  background-repeat: no-repeat;
}
.photobox a img {
  border: none;
}
```

You may have also noticed the subtle drop shadow effect in the borders of the image. The right-hand side of this drop shadow is actually part of the <div> tag's background image. Even though the images being displayed in this gallery are generally around 500 pixels tall, the <div> tag's background image is actually 800 pixels in height and includes a shadow that runs all the way down its right-hand side. When this background is displayed in the page, the shadow appears to the right-hand side of the image, but the shadow is cut off by the background image of the link element, which is why it's not visible on the rendered page.

Similar CSS techniques using multiple background images can be used to create almost any edging effect imaginable, from scalloped edges like my stamp border, to gradient drop shadows. All it takes is an idea and a little ingenuity.

Any edge effect will help to bring more attention to an image, whether it's applied to that image directly using Photoshop, using a CSS background image, or using CSS borders. The most important thing to remember is that borders and edge effects should enhance the images they surround, not drown them out. Avoid adding a border that calls more attention to itself than to the photo it's highlighting.

Application: Polishing off Florida Country Tile

While Ed was very happy with the web page designs, his main feedback about the comps I showed him was that the image didn't look like it was taken in the city in which his company operates. I explained that neither of the header images I used in the comps were actually taken locally, and that those were really just placeholder images. I also let him know that they were stock images, so if he did want to use them, they were available. He really liked the homepage design with the image of the beach at sunrise, though, even after I explained that, according to the description in iStockphoto, the picture was actually of a sunset at Malibu—it's shown in Figure 5.33.

After that, the conversation turned to web site content and the photos of his work that he wanted to include in the web site's gallery. Ed said that he'd taken some pictures with his digital camera of a few tile and countertop installations but wasn't sure which ones should go on the web site, or which would even be usable. I told him what I tell every other client about content photos—the more, the merrier. Even if you only have room for a limited number of images, it's better to pick them from a large pool of images than to have just enough

Figure 5.33: The beach image I used in the homepage comp

and not be able to eliminate any. Additionally, having several shots of the same area helps to create a visual reference, and allows you to show different levels of detail. The images of the marble countertops in Figure 5.34 are great examples of the kind of thing I'm talking about.

Figure 5.34: Three images of the same countertop

While each of these images shows a different angle of the marble countertop on this kitchen island, they also show increasing detail as the camera moves closer to the actual counter surface. By showing all three of these images together in a gallery, viewers will be able to gain a much better understanding of dimension, scale, and, most importantly, how a similar material might look in their own kitchen designs. Also, an image like the one on the far right might be too ambiguous to use alone. When placed alongside the other two images, though, it's easily recognizable and helps to validate the others.

Figure 5.35: Original tub image

Some of the images that Ed sent me were usable, but in need of a little tweaking. The marble tub deck in Figure 5.35 is definitely such a candidate.

It's obvious that this photo focuses mainly on the tub and the marble decking around it, which Florida Country Tile installed, but there are a few aspects of this image that detract from its beauty. If we want the tub to be the center of attention, we'll need to apply some of the rules of emphasis we talked about in Chapter 1.

To begin with, there's too much going on around the tub itself. While Florida Country Tile also installed the custom tile work in this bathroom, this photo captures only a minor part of the flooring and, therefore, doesn't do it justice. The toilet that's creeping in on the right-hand side of the image also adds a level of distraction.

Figure 5.36: Tub image without surrounding distractions

When I crop out these unsightly details, the tub becomes a much more solid focal point, as Figure 5.36 shows. However, as I crop this image, I make one intentional decision that makes the tub less of a focal point. Rather than cropping the windows down to a point at which the tub would be centered in the composition, I crop them to the nearest windowpane divider. This helps the image to feel more balanced.

The only other aspects that bother me about this image are the dust on the marble and the view out the windows. If I'd been the one taking the pictures, I'd have wiped that dust away with my shirt, if necessary, to prevent my having to Photoshop it out later. Fortunately, a combination of the Stamp tool and the Burn tool helps me get rid of most of the gray haze. My problem with the view is that the beautiful river scene outside the windows is almost completely whited out due to the lack of light in the room. To improve this situation, I use the Polygonal Lasso tool to select all eight panes of glass, and then increase the saturation

and contrast levels a little. Now you can clearly see the palm fronds, river channel, and mangrove trees from this second-floor bathroom window—as Figure 5.37 shows.

Figure 5.37: Tub image with less dust and an improved river view

While every image in the gallery could use this kind of individual attention, it might not be practical for me to edit each image, especially if there are a lot of them. The best thing to do is to look for the pictures that have the most potential, and improve those few images. In Florida Country Tile's case, these improved images can now be used elsewhere in the site's content.

If you're working with non-professional photography, you're bound to have some images that make you cringe. Perhaps the lighting is bad, the focus is blurry, or the angle is wrong. Either way, you know the moment you look at it that this is a photo that will not be making its way onto the web site. Before you toss these kinds of photos aside, though, ask yourself if you can use the image in some other way. Take the shower stall image in Figure 5.38. While it's obvious that the creamy ceramic and shiny glass tiles are an excellent combination for a bathroom wall, this photo looks almost accidental. The good thing that I see in this image, though, is the texture of the glass tiles. The contrast and variation of each individual tile gives it a very natural look. By taking that texture and using it in a fun and unexpected way, I can leverage the idea of the tile, tying it into a totally different

Figure 5.38: Is that a ... shower stall?

scene. Just for fun, I decide to use that texture as a translucent overlay on a Florida mangrove scene, bringing in the "Country Tile Understands Your Florida Style" tagline that I used in the homepage header image. While this image, which is shown in Figure 5.39, isn't wide enough to use as a header, it shows the creative possibilities that combined imagery can have.

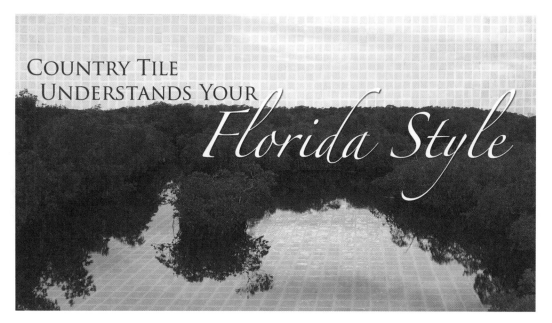

Figure 5.39: The glass tile texture from the previous image overlaid on a photo of some mangrove trees

Coming up with the content imagery and the final graphics for a web site design is all about taking the lessons of graphic design theory and applying them in large and small ways to each page of a site. Try to keep the target audience engaged with relevant and interesting imagery, but also remember to let the content speak for itself. As a designer, it's easy for me to get caught up in the individual pixels, and the eye candy of web site design, but it's important to keep in mind the fact that content is king. As you move on from the pure design phase to developing your site in HTML, it's crucial to maintain this content-centric focus.

Finding Inspiration (or Don't Always Follow the Crowd)

One of the most exciting things about being a designer at this point of the Web's evolution is the sense of community and interaction that has developed among web professionals. On every design-related news site, blog, or forum, there are always people who are willing to share their opinions and techniques. While the design community is an invaluable resource, it can sometimes be an unnecessary crutch. I'm always looking for new sources of inspiration and because there are so many authoritative designers out there who offer their ideas and portfolios online, it would be easy for me to find all the inspiration I need from my fellow web site designers. In and of itself, that isn't such a bad thing, but if every web designer was getting his or her ideas from other web designers, eventually everybody would have all the same ideas.

While the design principles and guidelines we've discussed through this book can help you make aesthetically pleasing and practical design decisions, they're no substitute for character and originality. The most important thing you can bring to the design table is your own personality, experiences, and interests. These three resources should form the foundations of your design work. If every designer spent less time trying to emulate the latest design trends and more time defining his or her own style, the Web would be a much more interesting place. While I'd love to be able to tell you how to define your own style, that's something I'm continually trying to learn for myself. I wish you the best of luck in your future design endeavors, and hope you've found this book to be both helpful and encouraging as you kick off a career—or hobby—in web design.

Index

A

achromatic color scheme 51
additive color model 46–8
adjustments, imagery
  cropping 140–2, 144–5, 160
  Photoshop 143–7, 160–2
aesthetic perspective, defining
    good design 4–6
aged style, texture 85–7
alpha channel, imagery 149
amesnjas web site, imagery
    156–8
analo-adjust color scheme 58
analogous color scheme 52–3
anatomy of a letterform,
    typography 104–6
appeal, imagery 131
application example
  color schemes 62–6
  design process 32–6
  Florida Country Tile 32–6,
    62–6, 91–7, 125–8, 159–62
  imagery 159–62
  texture 91–7
  typography 125–8
associations, color 39–43
asymmetrical balance 14–15

B

background
  browsers 81
  pattern 78–83, 92–5
balance 12–15
  asymmetrical 14–15
  symmetrical 12–13
big type style, texture 88–90
bilateral symmetry 13
black, color associations 43
blink tag 22

blockquote element, emphasis
    22
blue, color associations 41–2
border drop shadows, CSS
    155–6, 158
borders
  CSS 154–6
  imagery 149–58
  stamp-style 149, 151–2
bread-and-butter layouts 22–4
brightness, imagery 145
browsers
  background 81
  file formats 148–9
bulleted list, typography
    126–7
Bus Full of Hippies template 5
business cards, starting point
    1, 32

C

cartoon style, texture 87–8
character, inspiration 163
choosing fonts 120–4
choosing imagery 159–62
clipart, imagery 139–40
CMYK subtractive color model
    46–8
Colly web site 30
color 38–66
  additive color model 46–8
  associations 39–43
  cool 44
  hexadecimal notation 59–62
  intensity 45
  palettes 59–66
  primary 46–8
  psychology 38–43
  saturation 45
  secondary 46–8

shade 45, 49–51, 63–4
subtractive color model 46–8
temperature 44, 63–4
tertiary 46–8
theory 101; 46–7
tint 45, 49–51, 63–4
value 45
warm 44
wheels 46–8
color schemes 49–58
  achromatic 51
  analo-adjust 58
  analogous 52–3
  application example 62–6
  changing 53
  complementary 54–6, 63–4
  discordant 56
  double complementary
    57–8, 64
  Florida Country Tile 62–6
  generators 60–2
  mono-split-complement 58
  monochromatic 49–51
  monochromatic with mo'
    pop 58
  simultaneous contrast 56
  split-complementary 57–8
  tetradic 57–8, 64
  triadic 57–8
  variants 58
communication
  defining good design 4–6
  design process 2–3
  typography 98
comp (comprehensive
    dummy), design process
    2, 4
complementary color scheme
    54–6, 63–4
consistency, defining good
    design 6

DELIVER
FIRST CLASS
WEB SITES

101 ESSENTIAL CHECKLISTS
BY SHIRLEY KAISER

101 CHECKLISTS FOR WEB DESIGN, USABILITY, SEO, AND MORE

THE CSS
ANTHOLOGY

101 ESSENTIAL TIPS, TRICKS & HACKS

BY RACHEL ANDREW

THE MOST COMPLETE QUESTION AND ANSWER BOOK ON CSS

BUILD YOUR OWN
WEB SITE
THE RIGHT WAY
USING
HTML & CSS
BY IAN LLOYD

LEARNING HTML AND CSS HAS NEVER BEEN SO MUCH FUN!

sitepoint®

THE
PHOTOSHOP
ANTHOLOGY

101 WEB DESIGN TIPS, TRICKS & TECHNIQUES

BY **CORRIE HAFFLY**

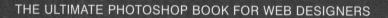

THE ULTIMATE PHOTOSHOP BOOK FOR WEB DESIGNERS